WHAT *I* ALWAYS KNEW, BUT NOW *I* KNOW

WHAT *I* ALWAYS KNEW, BUT NOW *I* KNOW

TERESA L. KELSO

XULON PRESS

Xulon Press
2301 Lucien Way #415
Maitland, FL 32751
407.339.4217
www.xulonpress.com

Printed in the United States of America.

ISBN-13: 978-1-5456-7925-8

THIS BOOK IS DEDICATED TO:

My heavenly Father. Thank You for dying on the cross for me and taking my sin so I can be free. Thank You for all my blessings, which none I have earned. Thank You for all my family and friends. Thank You for all my "God-sends" to show me Your love; I am honored and humbled. Thank You for loving me unconditionally. Thank You for the miracles You send. Thank You for allowing me the choice of eternal life with You. Thank You, I love You.

My beautiful and loving mom. Thank you for the inspiration you have been to me for as long as I can remember. Thank you for all the love and nurturing you taught me. You were there to change my diapers, for the haircut I hated, when I got my first training bra, when the homework piled up, when the pregnancy came, when the wedding came, and when the marriage went. You were there when my kids needed a coat and when I needed a loan. You have always been there for me, but the biggest one is your love. It's like no other besides Jesus. Thank you, I love you.

My amazing dad. Thank you for teaching me about life and the dos and the don'ts. Thank you for showing me what hard work and dedication are. You taught me how to pick a watermelon, and you always taught me if I'm going to do it, do it right; and if I use it, put it back where I got it. Dad, I never wanted the day to come that arrived on May 31, 2010. I find myself realizing how much I miss you and would love to hear your "hello, Sis." I look forward to the day that I can once again hear those words. Until then, I will just remember what you have shared with me. Thank you, I love you.

My three sisters: Sheryl, Darnell, and Vickie. I love you and appreciate each of you. Darnell (Nelly) I miss you so much. You were as unique of a sister as they come, which made you who you were. We sisters have not only a sister bond, but a friendship I wouldn't change for the world. You have taught me to appreciate myself and know my worth. I am proud to say we are not only sisters here on earth, but we are sisters in Christ Jesus, and that means we are sisters for eternity. Thank you, I love you.

My two brothers: Kenny and Curtis. You both have been such amazing brothers. You have protected me, and you have saved me financially when you didn't even know it—all those times I received a card with money in it that always seemed to come when I needed it the most, all the fresh eggs and fresh lamb, and a home bought for me with pure love, and for just being there with all your love and support. Thank you, I love you.

My husband Eric. Even though our marriage is quite unique, I admire you and I am proud of you. I have learned a lot from you that I will carry with me the rest of my life. I adore your whole family, especially Momma Josie, and I have enjoyed all of our family get-togethers through the years; they are cherished memories in my heart forever. Thank you, I love you.

My eight wonderful children Sarah, Lacey, Devyn, and Sky and my four stepchildren, Travis, Angie, Ryan, and

Frankie. You guys are all amazing adults. I am so proud of you and I love you. It gives me great joy to look into your eyes and to see your smiles. Thank you for being the joy of my life. I pray for each one of you that God will lead your path and that you will be healthy and happy and have a beautiful life surrounded by love from your own children and children to come. Thank you for loving me back and making my life complete. Thank you, I love you.

My ten-plus grandkids that Grammy loves so much: Jesse, Riley, Zakri, Edwin, Alyssa, Maliah, Jovon, Elsa, Dream, and Sophia; extended family grandkids: Joshua, Miranda, Napo Jr., Nadia, and Max; and great-grandkids: Yelena and Analeah. You are the greatest kids ever, and I am proud of each one of you for your own special and amazing talents and just for who you are, uniquely designed by God. I am so blessed because of you. Thank you, I love you.

My grandparents, aunts, uncles, nieces and nephews, and all my beautiful cousins. To my many extended family members, my loving and wonderful friends, and my brothers and sisters in Christ. You all have made my life much brighter. Thank you, I love you.

Table of Contents

THIS BOOK IS DEDICATED TO: vii

SPECIAL THANK YOU TO:. xv

A Poem for My Mom Tillie xx

What I Always Knew, but Now I Know #1 1

Little Things in Life. 5

HEAVENLY Chocolate Chip Cookies. 7

What I Always Knew, but Now I Know #2 9

A Friend 11

God-Send by Devyn Williams 13

Rainbow Hug 17

WASHED Fluffy Cranberry Cheese Pie. 17

What I Always Knew, but Now I Know #3 19

MERCY Mexican Turkey Roll-Ups. 25

Answers to Quiz "How Smart Are You?" 26

Some Interesting Bible Facts. 27

Love Never Fails 29

Our American Heritage Written by Herbert Leon
Hatcher, 1956. 29

The Lord's Love and Protection 33

COURAGE Brown-Bag Burrito. 33

A Daily Prayer for Protection 34

What I Always Knew, but Now I Know #4 36

What I Always Knew, but Now I Know #5 38

    A Prayer for Good Health. 39

    Losing Life to Find the Soul 42

    Child in His Arms 42

    Moving Mountains 42

    On the Mount of Olives 42

    Sermon on the Mount 43

    The Lord's Prayer. 44

    Sometimes Love Hurts. 44

    Friends Strengthen Us 44

What I Always Knew, but Now I Know #6 45

    HOLY Basil Olive Dip 49

    A HELPFUL HINT 50

    Major Accomplishments. 54

    References 54

    I Am a Christian 55

    Recipe for a House of Love 56

    The Journey 56

    Letting Go Can Be Easy, or It Can Be Hard. 57

    FAITHFUL Fish Tacos 59

    A HELPFUL HINT 61

    God's Love Letter to You 62

What I Always Knew, but Now I Know #7 64

    GUARDIAN Angel Food Cake 66

I Have a Friend Named Jesus 67

The Gift of Friendship. 67

Friends Like Us 68

Friendship 68

What I Always Knew, but Now I Know #8 70

A Smile. 71

A Wing and a Prayer 74

The Words to Say I Love You. 75

HOPE Greek Grilled Catfish 75

What I Always Knew, but Now I Know #9 77

In Loving Memory of Darnell Elaine Hatcher (Knapp)
December 31, 1955–November 22, 1996 79

What I Always Knew, but Now I Know #10 82

** A HELPFUL HINT ** 88

What I Always Knew, but Now I Know #11 93

What I Always Knew, but Now I Know #12 95

Rest for Your Souls 96

I Am a New Creation in Him. 96

What I Always Knew, but Now I Know #13 97

Wings Of An Angel. 99

God's Only Son 99

What I Always Knew, but Now I Know #14 102

Today I Saw Him. 103

What I Always Knew, but Now I Know #15 107

Poem Written by Devyn Williams. 110

What I Always Knew, but Now I Know #16 113

What I Always Knew, but Now I Know #17 121

What I Always Knew, but Now I Know #18 132

What I Always Knew, but Now I Know #19 152

Some Questions for Thought. 163

We Need Jesus Now More Than Ever. 165

What I Always Knew, but Now I Know #20 166

Just a little color fun, from Color Wheel Pro. 171

GRACE Bacon-and-Cheese Breakfast Pizza 180

Ten Fun Facts for You. 181

Did You Know ... ?. 182

SALVATION Lemon-Herb Salmon 185

God, Forgive Me When I Whine. 185

Don't Quit. 187

ABOUT THE AUTHOR 195

SPECIAL THANK YOU TO:

Sister Sheryl for encouraging me to write from way back when, and words to support it.

Sister Vickie for giving me encouraging words of support and excitement.

My Daughter Sarah for the perfect picture from your beach trip for the cover.

My Daughter Lacey forbeing the biggest and best fighter ever. I love you.

Jessica, for all your love an dedication and being the best nurse to Lacey. I love you.

Amanda, for your strength, love and perseverance. I love you.

My friend Tony W. For your lifelong friendship I deeply appreciate, and all your help you have always given me.

My friend Ronnie C. for always being there when I needed you at a moments notice and for always being on time.

My friend Renee E. who sends with love just the right scripture when I need it the most.

My friend Connie D. who resights just the right scripture when I need it and has given of her time to help and create this books cover.

Special Thank you to my cousin Jeannie for keeping me on my toes by asking for updates on this book every step of the way.

All of the publishing team for your help, support, and patience with me through this wonderful experience.

This book is filled with true, amazing God-sends—inspirational poems, quizzes, little Bible studies, some recipes, and hopefully some uplifting and encouraging words. I hope in some way this book may give you an up-close and personal look at who Jesus is and what He can do in your life. Maybe it will inspire you to pursue your God-given talents, or it will touch your heart in some way to help you know the love of our Lord. Or possibly, it will give just the right truth of a Bible verse to give you hope and faith to trust that there is a God and He loves you unconditionally. God promises you the free gift of eternity. The question is, Will you love God back and accept His gift? From the core of my heart to the depth of my soul, I pray that in some way or another, this book will help lead you on a journey to understand how mighty and great our God and Savior is.

What I Always Knew, but Now I Know. I always knew God was real, but now I know He is. The name of this book couldn't have been anything but this. Through all the divine interventions I have experienced, those have always been the words I have said every time. It couldn't have been a more fitting title. This is my story, but God is the author.

I was so excited to write this book that I could hardly stand it. When I first started thinking about writing a book, before words were ever put on paper, I knew I wanted the book to be encouraging. I hope it is. I was hoping I knew enough or had been through enough to fill a book, but most of all, I wanted to show you how beautiful and amazing God is in all the splendor and majesty that describes Him. I have had some billboard moments that seem wild and crazy, but I am telling you, they are true and amazing God-sends. I pray you won't dismiss what I am saying, because if you haven't already had your own billboard moments, get ready! They are on their way because you, too, can experience your own God-sends if you will just believe. My relationship with the Lord has grown and continues to grow every day, and now I do have enough for this book and more. Thank You, Jesus!

Our lives are filled with so many amazing and wonderful miracles, and they begin with us, our very own births, for we are all God's children. Each of us is a special creation, and God says, "I have summoned you by name, you are mine" (Isaiah 43:1). With that being said, let me begin my story.

My name is Teresa, and I was born and raised in Lancaster, California. My mother is one of twelve children, and my father one of nine. I am the youngest of six children, all of us within nine years. Needless to say, I am blessed with a very large family and I love it. I myself have eight children: three biological, one adopted, and four stepchildren. I am also very proud and blessed to be called Grammy by my ten-plus grandchildren ranging from fifteen years down to three months old. They all have their own special talents that I am extremely proud of, and they are awesome individuals that I love so much.

I myself have played the flute since I was ten, and I still play from time to time. I enjoy it and want to think I have a pretty neat talent myself; of course, if you ask someone else, they may have a different opinion on that. I love to crochet and have made over forty blankets and have given them all away to family, friends, and even a few people I didn't know at a senior center. Can you tell I really enjoy crocheting? I have never even made a blanket for myself!

With encouragement being the purpose of this book, and to share with you my personal stories of what I always knew, but now I know, I want to encourage you to trust God today. He knows what you're going through, and He has a plan for your life. No matter what the circumstances may be, God is by your side and will see you through. It's pretty amazing when you think about it, that we get to spend as much time with God as we want. We have an open invitation of having the creator of the universe in our lives. What an absolute gift!

We need to always remember that enjoying life begins with enjoying yourself. You're the one person you're never going to get away from, so you'd better learn to like yourself. The expression *nobody's perfect* is so true. I'm not perfect, you're not perfect, but God is perfect.

Hopefully, though, we are on our way toward the goals God has given us and wants for us. The important thing to remember is that even though we are not perfect, we are still on a journey and we are loved. I thank God every day that I'm not where I need to be, but I'm not where I used to be either. That is beyond important for me to remember.

I have been in some very bad places in my life, some very low and dark places, but through the mercy and love of the Lord, He has pulled me out and given me another chance to do better and continue on. I know with all my heart God is not upset with me. In fact, I know He's probably pleased with me for trying to stay on His path. If I just try to keep on keeping on, God will be pleased with my desire to please Him.

I'm sure there will be times when I feel defeated, but that's part of the process. Growing and sometimes learning can be very challenging, but those good changes make us better people.

Enjoy yourself while you're going through the process of changing and growing and becoming more like Christ. Just keep saying, "God, I trust You. Even when I don't know what the outcome will be, I trust You, I trust You." All things work together for our good and for those who are called according to His design and purpose (Romans 8:28).

Isn't it delightful to spend time with people who can be light-hearted and encouraging? Their humor and their positive nature are infectious. It is so much more satisfying to laugh than to be miserable. If you think about how blessed you are, it will help you to focus on the words *too blessed to be stressed*. I try to remember to answer like that when I'm greeted and someone asks me how I am. "A happy heart is good medicine and a cheerful mind works, but a broken spirit dries up the bones" (Proverbs 17:22).

Something my mom always says and it's awesome:

> "Do your giving while you're living so you're knowing where it's going."

Speaking of Momma Tillie, here is a poem I wrote for her:

A Poem for My Mom Tillie

Because of you, Mom, I know what love is.
It's patient, it's sacrificing, it's sharing joy and keeping faith,
It's what makes us strong and helps us find our way.

Because of you, Mom, I know what family is.
It's laughing, it's learning, it's being real and being friends,
And that love is there no matter what.

Because of you, Mom, I know about the heart.
I know what's at the heart of a good life—love and family,
Loving the Lord and appreciating yourself.

Because of you, Mom, I know what empathy is.
To feel for others and pray for them,
And to know and love Jesus makes a difference.

Because of you, Mom, I am who I am today.
I know my value and I know my worth,
And I'm a lady who loves the Lord with all my heart.

Because of you, Mom, I am so blessed.
You have taught me to count each and every one of them.
All these things I cherish, Mom, because of you.

Thank you, Mom. I love you!

Dear Mom, I love you more than words can begin to say. The appreciation and admiration I have for you and for all you've done for me cannot begin to touch the surface of anything I have to offer back to you. Mom, you have seen me through good times, bad times, and happy and sad times, and you have loved me through it all. You have guided me, protected me, encouraged me, and stood by me through every adventure in my life. You haven't always agreed with me, and at times have been disappointed in me, but through it all you have loved me. You have been my rock and my best friend, and now that I have been given the gift of being a mom, I appreciate you, my mother, even that much more. Mom, I will never stop looking to you for guidance, direction, and advice. I can't express how blessed I feel and how grateful I am to God for giving me the most precious mom anyone could have asked for. This is not meant just for today, but for *always.* Again and again, thank you, Mom, and, thank you, my God!

I would not want to count the times in my life that I have let some dumb, minor nothing ruin my day. It has taken me a while, but with God's help, I have learned not to take everything in life so seriously. It's so important to have fun and laugh. You would be surprised how that will decrease your stress. Some things in my life have been so funny that I have thought about them again and again, and each time they have brought a smile to my face, and I have even laughed over and over just thinking about them. I could be all alone, and all of sudden I think of something funny that happened and it cracks me up all over again. What a joy!

Speaking of joy, we all have the option to have joy in our lives; we just need to choose it.

The joy of the Lord can ease any emotional and physical pain and bring a new level of satisfaction in life. Here is a little something I came across somewhere that I thought was kind of cute: A little boy was scolded in school. The teacher told him, "You must not laugh out loud in the classroom." The little boy responded, "I'm sorry, teacher. I didn't mean to, but I was smiling and my smile busted."

No matter what you are going through in life, if you remember "the joy of the Lord is your strength" (Nehemiah 8:10), you will have a smile on your face no matter how big your situation is. When you feel life is too stressful, just pray that your smile will bust. Be thankful you can laugh as you trust God to take care of those problems. With God's help, you can become a person whose first response is faith not fear, joy and not sorrow.

The next time you feel your peace slipping away and stress picking up, take a moment to stop and remember the benefits you've been given as a child of God. The benefits of this mind-set aren't something we earn by impressing God; they are things He freely gives us because we are His children and He loves us. Always remember God's goodness. It's so easy to forget if we don't stay focused.

What you think about and what you focus on are going to affect how you see life. If you focus on God's goodness, that His promises are true, pure, loving, kind, and gracious, you won't be as frustrated and discouraged and fed up with the difficulties in life. Thankfully, the Lord has begun to teach me how to set my attention on the good things in my life, and with God's help, I have begun to see that I don't have to let daily problems and inconveniences determine my happiness any longer. When I started taking the time to focus on God's goodness and His blessings in my life, my outlook on life has definitely changed. My attitude improved, and I saw a joy I didn't have before. So I try really hard to stay focused on God's positive things in my life, and it gives me a sense of perspective, stability, thankfulness, and balance.

"Fix your eyes on Jesus, the pioneer and perfecter of faith" (Hebrews 12:2).

"Set your minds and keep it set on what is above— the higher things, not on the things that are on earth" (Colossians 3:2).

One of the biggest downfalls I have is focusing on the negative things that are happening to me and around me and letting those things fill my heart with frustration, fear, and anxiety. That's why I am so thankful that I am practicing setting my attention on the good things in my life. Now when I'm faced with a situation that used to drive me bananas, by the grace of God I am learning to keep my joy, trust God, and keep moving forward.

That is why I decided to write this book. I can't wait to share with you what the Lord has shown me and is still showing me. God has promised that He is with you and that He will never leave your side (Deuteronomy 31:6)." If God is with you, you have no obstacle worth stressing about. God's not going to let you sink; He is in control, and He will see you to the other side". "Be not grieved and depressed, for the joy of the Lord is your strength" (Nehemiah 8:10). Wouldn't it be wonderful if, as you read these words, an angel whispered in your ear of God's unconditional love for you? You may be able to hear it if you listen carefully. We must never make the mistake of blaming ourselves for not validating certain happenings in life, for only God knows the answer to the ultimate mysteries of life and death.

You know what I've heard the Bible stands for? **Bible—** **B**asic **I**nformation **B**efore **L**eaving **E**arth. And what does faith stand for? **Faith—For Always I Trust Him.** Something to think about, huh?

Have you ever noticed that when we reach out to one another in faith, something wonderful happens? It's like when we reach out to other people, we also find that we are reaching up to God and God is reaching down to us. Part of all the good we do draws close to our hearts like a whispered prayer in our ear.

I would like to share my personal experiences of how God has shown me in His own way that He is real and He loves me. This is what I always knew, but now I know!

What I Always Knew, but Now I Know #1

W hen I was about ten or eleven, my mom gave me a silver ring with a ribbon-like design. I loved that ring. It was from a company called Sarah Coventry jewelry, a pretty popular jewelry company back then, almost as popular as Avon. I'm sure you've heard of them. I wore the ring all the time; I was pretty proud of it.

Let's fast forward six or seven years. I was now in high school and had met a boy named David. David and I became boyfriend and girlfriend, without the approval of my parents, of course. They did not like it at all, especially because David was a few years older than I was. Still without their approval or consent, I continued to date David. I was so in love. You know how it is—your first love, you just feel so in love. Well, I was no different. I kept thinking about that ring my Mom had given me and was thinking, *Do I dare have the ring engraved to say* David *on one ribbon and* Teresa *on the other ribbon*?

I had my own money because I had worked a summer job at Fosters Freeze, so I didn't have to ask my parents for money, which, if I would have needed money from them, I most likely would not have been blessed with that money. Remember, they were not in agreement with my relationship. My dad would often say, "You are too young; you have your whole life for that stuff." I'm sure my parents were right, but don't we think we know it all at that age?

1

Without my parents' approval once again, I had the ring engraved with *David* on one ribbon and *Teresa* on the other, just as I had wanted.

I was now seventeen, almost eighteen, and my parents' biggest fear happened: I became pregnant. I was so afraid to tell my parents. I think the thought in my mind was I would rather be dead than to tell them, especially my dad, that I was pregnant (which I thought I would be dead anyway when he found out). Well, to my surprise, of course they were devastated and upset with me, but as you can see, they didn't kill me. Thank You, Jesus!

My mom asked me, "Well, what are you planning to do?" and I answered her, "What do you mean?" I was thinking she meant to get an abortion. I would have never agreed to that, but that was not where she was going with that at all. She meant, when was I getting married? I was shocked. Married? What? But I guess if you're going to play like an adult, then you better grow up now, so I grew up and grew up fast. I was going to be a mommy.

Well, my body was starting to change. I was starting to get puffy, weight was coming on, and jewelry was now coming off, fingers too swollen to wear any rings right now. Into the jewelry box they went. My tummy was getting big, and it was getting closer to knowing what the sex of the baby was going to be. *Yay! It's a girl. Gee, what should I name her?* I had no names picked out and had never even given a thought to what I would name my first baby, girl or boy. I went and bought one of those baby-name books, trying to decide on a name.

My brother Curtis, who is next in line to me, one day said, "Sis, do you have a name picked out yet"? I told him no, and he said, "Could I name her?"

I said, "Well, it depends on what name you're talking about, brother."

He said, "There is a song from Fleetwood Mac Called "Sara".

I told him, "I like that name; it's pretty. Okay, Sarah it is." So I named my baby girl Sarah. But with the letter H at the end.

Fast forward about ten years. Sarah was now ten, and I thought now would be a great time to pass on the silver ribbon ring to my daughter. I hadn't worn it for years; in fact, since I was too swollen to wear it while I was pregnant, that was the last time it had been out of the jewelry box.

I got the ring from my jewelry box and gave it to Sarah. I told her, "Years ago I had this ring engraved with your dad's name and my name when we were dating, and I thought you would like it."

She said, "Oh, how neat, Mom. Thank you."

I told her, "Maybe if you still have it when you have kids, you can pass it on."

She was grinning and really checking out the ring. She said, "Mom, that's so neat that it has my dad's name, your name, and mine. Thank you."

3

I said, "What do you mean?" and she said, "Look, Mom, my name is on the back."

I about fell over. I couldn't believe my eyes; on the back of the ring was my daughter's name. Remember, it was a Sarah Coventry ring, with the name spelled the same way. Who but God would have known that I would get pregnant at seventeen with a baby girl my brother named Sarah after one of his favorite songs, and the ring contained all three of our names on it ten years prior to the event? Is that not amazing?

Sometimes we become so involved with the business of living that we often lose sight of the author of life. We sometimes wonder if God is even there. Then we think about His plan for us, and how the signs and clues He sends us are simply amazing, and then we know He is there. He has His reasons for doing what He does when He does it, and I pray someday He might explain them to me. But until then, I trust Him.

A few things to keep in mind and remember: Remember, there are few things in life more stressful than thinking it's all on your shoulders. Remember that God is good and it is His desire that you place your trust completely in Him. Remember, if you'll do what you can do, God will do the rest. Remember, you don't get to choose what happens around you, but you do get to choose how you respond to it. Remember, loving others is the only way to keep the God-kind of life flowing through you.

God's love is a gift to us. It's in us, but we need to release it to others through words and actions. Remember, peace and happiness don't happen by accident. These are choices you get to make. Remember to trust God in the midst of trying times. He knows what you're going through. He hasn't left you, because He has a plan for your life. We always give Him the big things, but do we give Him the little things too? Remember, when faced with a decision, going to God should be the first option, not the last resort.

Little Things in Life
Little things in life, too often we don't realize
What we have until it's gone.
Too often we wait too late to say, "I'm sorry; I was wrong."
Sometimes it seems we hurt the ones we hold dearest
    to our hearts,
And we allow stupid things to tear our lives apart.
Far too many times we let unimportant things get
    in our mind,
And by then it's usually too late to see what made us blind.
So be sure you let people know how much they
    mean to you;
Take the time to say the words before your time is through.
Be sure that you appreciate everything you've got,
And be thankful for the little things in life that mean a lot!

Prayer is very personal and intimate. It's like a marriage, only it's with God. Sometimes we get confused, but, "God's voice thunders in marvelous ways and He does great things beyond our understanding" (Job 37:5). Prayer can be a powerful weapon, a weapon that can help the ones we love. The Bible says that, "if we pray, we will receive" (Matthew 21:22). "Our prayers are powerful and effective" (James 5:16).

Do you know what *grace* means? It means there is nothing we can do to make God love us more or less. No amount of knowledge of the Bible, no amount of knowledge of how to pray, no amount of times we fail—God will never love us any more or any less. Grace means that God already loves us as much as an infinite God can possibly love. Grace in itself is a blessing that God has bestowed on us. It is not something we can earn or deserve. It's only because He loves us that we get God's best.

I am so grateful for all the blessings the Lord has poured into my life. I also appreciate the tough lessons and hardships I have experienced because they make me appreciate the blessings that come my way even more. Be careful not to focus only on the blessings received, but also on the blessings you give. We are people who love blessings. I mean, don't we bless each other when we sneeze, or bless each other when things go wrong, or when we eat? We are always looking for blessings in our lives; we are constantly on the lookout.

"Oh Lord, You bless the righteous and surround them with Your favor" (Psalm 5:12). When I think of God's blessings, I think of how He doesn't even have to do those things for us, yet He does them anyway because His love is unconditional.

When we are in a relationship, no matter what type of relationship it is, we need balance. But when people say it should be 50/50, I don't feel that way. I think it should be 100/100, because if it's 50/50, you're only giving half of what you have; when you give 100/100, however, you're giving your all. An Important fact~*If everyone would take care of someone else, then everyone would be taken care of~*. Please, read that line again!

— — — ◆ — —

"A happy heart makes the wonderfully made; Your works are wonderful, I know that full well" (Psalm 139:14).

HEAVENLY Chocolate Chip Cookies

Ingredients:

4 cups all-purpose flour
2 teaspoons baking soda
1 tablespoon baking powder
1 teaspoon coarse salt
2 cups unsalted butter
2 cups brown sugar, packed
1 cup plus two tablespoons granulated sugar
2 large eggs
2 teaspoons real vanilla extract
1¼ pounds chocolate chips (semisweet, dark, or whatever you prefer)
Pinch of sea salt
Optional: pecans, dried cherries, or any dried berries

Directions:

Preheat oven to 350 degrees, and line a cookie sheet with parchment paper.

Mix the flour, baking soda, baking powder, and coarse salt in a bowl. Set aside.

In a mixer, cream butter and sugars together (about 5 minutes). Then add eggs, mixing well after each addition.

On low speed, add the dry ingredients (5–10 seconds). Drop in chocolate chips and/or pecans and cherries.

Scoop 36 half-golf-ball-sized cookies onto the baking sheet. Sprinkle with sea salt. Bake until golden brown but still soft, approximately 18–20 minutes.

Cool on a wire rack for 10 minutes. Serve warm, optionally with vanilla ice cream.

Makes approximately 36 cookies.

I would like to share another God-send I experienced. God is such an awesome God.

What I Always Knew, but Now I Know #2

used to work for a company called Western Studios, in the accounting department, several years back. I loved my job there. We stored all the props and scenery for movies. It was one of the best jobs I've ever had. I was very fortunate to be able to talk with many movie stars and entertainers. Just to name a few, I got to talk with Beyonce, Dick Clark, and Anita Baker, from whom I still have a signed letter thanking me for taking care of her account and keeping it on track. I felt so good about my compliments. I even received an award for collecting the most past-due accounts. I really must have loved my job!

One day on my way home from work, while I was getting off the freeway, something told me to stall at the green light, so I stalled at the green light. About that time there came a car flying through the red light, hitting another car and flipping it over. This happened right before my eyes. I started crying. I couldn't believe what had just happened, but by the grace of God, it wasn't me. I couldn't believe that I would have been that car if I would have not listened to that little voice speaking to me. Fortunately, the people in the car did survive, again by the grace of God. I drove the rest of the way home bawling and shaking and thanking Jesus. Oh my Lord, I was so grateful to God that He spared me from that accident and gave me the ability to pay attention to the divine intervention that I am convinced it was. God is so good, loving, and merciful. Thank You, Lord.

If our daily walk with the Lord is to be a close and intimate relationship, then we must share all things with Him no matter how ordinary. All of us know so little about God. Even when we look as far as we can into the power and perfection of His mighty ways, we have really seen just the fringes of God. God is absolutely complete in all His ways, in all He does within Himself. Nothing we do or don't do changes God in any way; He is still beyond our comprehension, and nothing in our universe compares to God. Knowing how mighty God is sure makes me feel mighty small, and to know how powerful God is sure makes me feel mighty powerless. To know how strong God is sure makes me feel mighty weak, and to know how much the God of the universe loves me sure makes me feel loved.

Here is a test to find out whether your mission on earth is finished: if you're alive, it isn't. Hmm.

I used to ask God to help me, but then as my heart began to change, I started asking Him how I might help Him. Miracles are momentary glimpses into a mystery of such power, depth, and beauty that if we were to see it head-on, we would likely question its reality.

I like to compare prayer to the wind. You can't actually see the wind, but you can feel it and see the results of it. It is kind of like as much of heaven is visible as we have eyes to see.

A Friend

A friend is someone we turn to when our spirits need a lift. A friend is someone we treasure, for their friendship is a gift. A friend is someone who fills our lives with beauty, joy, and grace and makes the world we live in a better and happier place. This goes out to all my past, present, and future friends that the Lord graciously has put in my path. Thank you!

When you gaze in awe, admiration, and wonder at something or someone, you begin to take on something of the character of the object of your worship.

—N. T. Wright

What comes into our minds when we think about God is the most important thing about us.

—A. W. Tozer

It's not the task of Christianity to provide easy answers to the question, but to make us progressively aware of a mystery. God is not so much the object of our knowledge as the cause of our wonder.

—K. Ware.

Why then did God give them free will? Because free will, though it makes evil possible, it is also the only thing that makes possible any love or goodness of joy worth having.

—C. S. Lewis

What I believe is so magnificent, so glorious, that it is beyond comprehension. To believe that the universe was created by a purposeful benign creator is one thing. To believe that this creator took on human vesture, accepted death and mortality, was tempted, betrayed, broken and all for the love of us defies reason. It is so wild that it terrifies some Christians who try to dogmatize their fear by lashing out at other Christians, because tidy Christianity with all answers given is easier than one which reaches out to wild wonder of God's love, a love we don't have to earn.

—M. L'Engle

Death leaves a heartache only God can heal, Love leaves a memory no one can steal.

—R. Puz

Sometimes I will be praying about something and I will feel the answers being processed. I sometimes get instant signs that somehow show me He is near and He hears me and He wants to show me we do have that connection. I just feel it in my heart.

—D. Williams.

God-Send by Devyn Williams

On a hot summer day in June just before noon, I was waiting for my wife, Amanda, to finish up a class that she was attending. I was sitting in my car in the parking lot, waiting and watching people go into different businesses. It was so

12

hot out, and I saw a homeless man sitting in front of the Dollar Tree store for about thirty minutes or so. He never once asked anyone for anything; He just sat there. He was the dirtiest homeless man I had ever seen in my life. He was dressed in the most tattered, raggediest clothes, and his shoes didn't even fit him. His feet were hanging out of them and were disgustingly dirty.

I watched so many people just walk right by him without even giving him a glance, let alone buy him food or a drink. It was breaking my heart to watch this. I felt drawn from my heart to go talk to this man and offer him something. He looked like he was really in a bad way and hungry. So I went over and I started talking to him. I proceeded to ask him if I could buy him a drink; I was sure he was thirsty, being as it was so hot. The way this man answered me "no" I will never forget. He had a unique accent like I had never heard before. I then asked him if he would like some food, and he answered me, "No, I am not hungry." The accent he used this time was different; it was as if he could speak any language. It gave me the chills. I then asked him if I could at least buy him some toiletries or give him some money, and with his unique accent he answered me, "No, my son. I have everything I need."

Those words he used and the way he said them made me feel strange, but I shouldn't really say "strange." I'll just say they made such peace and satisfaction came over me that I can't explain it. I walked back to my car, feeling chills rush through my body and in awe of this man's accent and answers.

Amanda came out, and I started the car and started to explain to Amanda what had just happened. I glanced over and looked at this man again, and he had tears streaming down his face. Then I felt a lump in my throat because I felt as if he was showing me he was pleased with my offerings. I again got chills all over. I am still amazed at that man and the way he answered and the accent he answered with. I feel in my heart it was some type of divine intervention or possibly even Jesus in disguise. You just never know!

This is the very reason we should be kind to strangers. Why? Because it could be an angel in disguise, but more than that, it could be Jesus in disguise to see if our hearts are loving and giving and nonjudgmental. If it's a test, are you going to pass it? Or would you flunk?

Maybe the next time a homeless person crosses your path, maybe you could just stop and say hello and wish them a blessed day. If they were standing there clean and in nice clothes, would you pass them by, or would you greet them? Don't let someone's outward appearance determine their inward spirit. If you don't know them, don't judge them. They still have a heart like you and me, and it breaks just like yours and mine, and it loves others just like yours and mine. Just always say to yourself, *What would Jesus do?* That helps you look into your heart and find the answer really fast.

Dear God, thank You that when I run out of strength, You do not. When I run out of wisdom, You give me encouragement. Thank You for the privilege of leaning on Your strong arms in times of need and quick decisions. Help me to trust in You every moment of every day. In Jesus' name, amen.

The power of Jesus is just as real today as it was back then. He can descend upon our hearts and give us everything we need in order to do what He calls us to do. In our modern world, we are filled with distractions that keep us from experiencing that wondrous cloud of God's presence in our lives. Time is often our worst enemy when it comes to living out our faith.

Each day we are faced with many decisions that will determine how we spend our time. This seems to be a battle that we never seem to master. I struggle sometimes with not spending enough valuable time with my Jesus. Without that I am nothing, and my priorities will go astray more and more each day.

The theme of "not I, but Christ" has begun to invade my heart, to creep into basically every thought and into almost every conversation. I'm beginning to understand the freedom those words offer to me. I have also started to open my eyes to the many things that clutter my life and threaten to keep me from the truth. I have also come face-to-face with my own faults in preventing God from being able to fully bless me and for me to feel a closeness with Him just from my own straying.

I'm sure you have asked yourself on many occasions, "Am I where I need to be on my journey with Jesus?" Probably we all have tried to spend more time with the Lord but fallen short due to spending too much time on trivial things that amount to nothing with value. We have to figure out the stuff in our lives that is preventing us or distracting us from making Christ first and being our all in all. Only our honesty, humility, and total dependence on Jesus will bring victory and honor.

What words of encouragement can you offer to someone going through a difficult time? I think the next time I'm asked,

I will start off by saying, "Not I, but Christ." That's the only answer I can give that holds any value. Christ can bring you through any situation because He is faithful and His promises are everlasting. I think that when we are not in tune with the Lord, we tend to get prideful. Pride is a danger in all our lives. Don't let pride be a priority. Let it go and let God.

Dear God, thank You for establishing priorities in my life. Thank You for the joy and fulfillment that comes when I follow Your plan for my life. Help me not to seek after temporal things like materialism, greed, and selfish pursuits. Help me instead to seek the things that will bring eternal fulfillment. In Jesus' name, amen.

Is it important to have "things" to be happy? Is it important to be lifted up on a pedestal? Is it important to focus on just work or just family? The answer is no. All these things will not be adequate to bring us joy unless we have God in our lives. Even though we find joy in these temporal activities, I can assure you, the enjoyment will be short-lived. At some point, these trivial things will lose their luster, and the hunger for a touch from Jesus will overwhelm you. That's when you know it's not your plan, but only God's plan for you that will work out. Value what God values and live your life accordingly.

Rainbow Hug
If I could catch a rainbow,
I would do it just for you,
And share with you its beauty
On the days you're feeling blue.
If I could build a mountain
You could call your very own,
A place to find serenity,

A place to be alone.
If I could take your troubles,
I would toss them in the sea,
But all these things I'm finding
Are impossible for me.
I cannot build a mountain
Or catch a rainbow anywhere,
But let me be what I know best,
A friend that's always there.

WASHED Fluffy Cranberry Cheese Pie

Ingredients:

Topping

1 package (3 ounces) raspberry-flavored gelatin
⅓ cup sugar
1¼ cups cranberry juice
1 can (8 ounces) jellied cranberry sauce
Filling
1 package (3 ounces) cream cheese, softened
¼ cup sugar
1 tablespoon milk
1 teaspoon vanilla extract
½ cup whipped topping
1 pastry shell (9 inches), baked

Directions:

In a mixing bowl, combine gelatin and sugar and then set aside. In a saucepan, bring cranberry juice to a boil.

17

Remove from the heat and pour over gelatin mixture, stir-ring until dissolved. Stir in the cranberry sauce. Chill until slightly thickened.

Meanwhile, in another mixing bowl, beat cream cheese, sugar, milk, and vanilla until fluffy. Fold in whipped top-ping. Spread evenly into pie shell.

Beat cranberry topping until frothy; then pour over filling. Chill overnight.

On to another amazing God-send experience!

What I Always Knew, but Now I Know #3

My son Devyn and I lived in a pretty little townhouse in Tujunga, California. It had a fireplace that I just loved, it had a wonderful view since we were on a hill, it had a two-car garage with an automatic garage-door opener, it was cozy and clean, and it was pretty close to my work and close to the school my son attended. It worked out perfectly, and we were very happy there. At this point in my story, we had already lived there for a year and a half.

I worked for a company called Jerry Leigh, the company that makes Disney clothing. It was another fun job I had, and the experience was great. On my hour lunch break, I used to go to a large alleyway where not many cars came through at that time of day, which was awesome because I got to eat my lunch in peace, read my Bible, and take a catnap before having to go back to work. It really helped me break up my day by getting away from the office for lunch, plus I enjoyed my "me time" where I could read my Bible and listen to my Christian station and all that—just "me time."

One day right before it was time to go back to work, I glanced over by a huge dumpster that was back there and noticed five huge bags filled to the top with what looked like stuffed animals. I walked over there, and sure enough, it was stuffed animals—five bags of brand-new stuffed animals! What the heck? I couldn't get over why anyone would just throw these animals away—they were new. I couldn't stand it and had a hundred ideas of what I could do with them, so I loaded them up in the back of my Explorer and back to work I went.

Over the next day or two, I made phone calls to different organizations to see if they would like the animals, but they all refused to take them. So I called the hospital, thinking they would love for the children's ward to get them, but again they said no, due to sanitary reasons. Then I called the convalescent hospital in Lancaster, where I grew up, and asked them if they would like the animals. They were so excited about them, and they said, "Sure. We would love for you to bring those. It would make the patients day." Perfect. I couldn't wait to take them and give them out.

The following weekend was going to be the perfect weekend to take them. For some reason, it was going to be a four-day weekend, and we were going to visit my mom in Lancaster anyway, so it was perfect. So there we were—the work-week had ended, and it was now Thursday, with the animals loaded and ready for delivery. I got home from work, my son got home from school, and we were ready to roll. We got into the car, and I raised the garage door, backed my Explorer out, and went to close the garage door, but the remote would not work. I tried it a few more times, but it still wouldn't work. I tried slapping the remote in my hand a few times, thinking maybe that would work. I tried taking the batteries out and changing them around, but that didn't work. In fact, nothing worked; I assumed the batteries must have died.

I got out of my car, went back into the garage to close it manually, and then had to come through the front door to get back to the car. To my unbelievable view, my front door

20

was wide open! What? I couldn't believe my eyes. I was so flabbergasted I started to cry. I couldn't believe that we would have left for four days and our front door would have been wide open the whole time. I couldn't stop crying and started to get chills all over my body, and suddenly I realized I had just experienced an intervention right before my very eyes. This had not happened by chance. God was looking out for us on our journey of giving.

I got back out to the car and was bawling like a baby, trying to explain to my son what had just happened. He couldn't believe the front door had been wide open. I started to back out again, and just because my curiosity got the best of me (even though I already knew in my heart what it was), I hit that remote again and the garage door went up and it went down, and it went up and it went down again. For another year and a half, that remote worked and that garage door went up and down just fine.

Wow! God's grace is absolutely amazing. When I think of that, I still get chills thinking at that very moment God knew what I, me, this girl in this big universe, needed at that very moment. I only have one word to describe it—*divine*.

"No eyes have seen, no ear has heard, no mind has conceived what God has prepared for those who love Him" (1 Corinthians 2:9). God hears us; He is everywhere, and whatever is in our minds and hearts He knows. Healing may be delayed because God is using difficulties in our lives to develop our spiritual muscles and to lift us to levels of understanding, compassion, and wisdom that might not otherwise be reached. What is initially considered a hardship might well turn out to be His invitation to grace and growth, and even a way to help others sometimes. We should rejoice and give thanks when difficulties occur, not because of the suffering itself, but because of what will come of it if we learn to trust God.

Think about all the miracles that He sends to us, beginning with the dawning of a new day. Life gets tough and things don't always work out as we hoped. Sometimes we wonder where God is, but when we have our own miracles of love and are able to reach out beyond ourselves to help the lives of others, when we seek the hopeful in difficult situations and try to build on it, when we love one another even in times when we can't see the good that love will do, we still need to Trust in God. He is there with you. God is so generous. As we remember and retell what He has done through testimonies, He's able and eager to do it again. There is so much truth to that. The more I share my testimony of my God-sends, the more He sends me.

I remember the first time I thought deeply about guardian angels and wondered if we have more than one, I realized God could send thousands of angels to assist me if that were His will. But more than that, I am encouraged to remember I'm always in God's care. He is more powerful than the angels. I think we are most familiar with the idea of angels protecting us, but that's not all they do. Angels also can deliver, guide, enlighten, or reveal information. When you think of how angels interact with believers, all you can say is wow!

God created the angels before he created anything else in the universe (Job 38:4–7).

All of the angels were created simultaneously (Matthew 22:30).

The number of angels is incomprehensible (Revelation 5:11).

Some angels rebelled against God (Isaiah 14).

Angels are powerful (2 Kings 19).

Angels were created to praise and worship God around His throne (Revelation 5:11–12).

Angels are charged with the responsibility of guiding the affairs of nations (Daniel 10).

Angels fight Satan and his demons until the victory is won at the end of time (Revelation 12:7–9).

Each church is assigned an angel to watch over it and help protect it (Revelation 1:20).

Angels will separate the wheat from the weeds at the final judgment (Matthew 12:38–42).

Angels minister to those who believe in Christ (Genesis 28:12).

Angels provide for physical needs of believers, as in the case of Elijah (1 Kings 19:5–7).

23

I wanted to show the amazement of angels and their works.

If you ever wonder where God is and whether He loves you, just think of this: if He loves you enough to take you to heaven when you die, why wouldn't He love you enough here on earth while you are alive? He calls us his sons and daughters. You know how we love our own children; God is no different, except His love for us is a perfect love, an unconditional love, a love that is forever.

I find it mighty fascinating that when God creates, He only has to speak the word. That's it and it's done. That's power! Your prayer, big or little, if it's given to Him in love and faith, He can, and will respond, and it is evident that He can bring something out of nothing if it pleases Him, and if it brings glory to his name. Nothing has ever made God more than He is.

How Smart Are *You*? (just a little fun quiz for you)

1. Do they have a fourth of July in England?
2. How many birthdays does the average man have?
3. Some months have thirty-one days; how many have twenty-eight?
4. How many outs are there in an inning?
5. Is it legal for a man to marry his widow's sister?
6. Divide thirty by half and add ten. What is the answer?
7. If there are three apples and you take away two, how many apples will you have?
8. The doctor gives you three pills and tells you to take one every half hour. How many minutes will they last?
9. A farmer has seventeen sheep. All but nine die. How many sheep does he have left?

10. How many animals of each sex did Moses take on the ark?
11. How many two-cent stamps are there in a dozen?

MERCY Mexican Turkey Roll-Ups

Ingredients:

2½ cups cubed cut turkey
1½ cups sour cream (divided)
3 teaspoons taco seasoning (divided into 1½ teaspoons)
1 can of cream of mushroom soup (divided)
1½ cups (6 ounces) shredded cheddar cheese (divided)
1 small onion chopped
½ cup salsa
¼ cup sliced ripe olives
10 flour tortillas (7 inches)
Shredded lettuce
Chopped tomatoes

Directions:

In a bowl, combine turkey, ½ cup sour cream, 1½ teaspoons taco seasoning, half of the soup, 1 cup of cheese, onions, salsa, and olives. Place ⅓ cup filling on each tortilla. Roll up and place seam side down in a greased 13-x 9-inch baking dish.

Combine remaining sour cream, taco seasoning, and soup, and pour over tortillas. Cover and bake at 350 degrees for 30 minutes or until heated through. Sprinkle with cheese.

Serve with shredded lettuce and chopped tomatoes. Top with additional salsa.

Makes about 5–6 servings.

Answers to Quiz "How Smart Are *You*?"

1. Yes, all countries have a July 4.
2. The average man has one birthday a year.
3. All months have the twenty-eighth.
4. There are six outs in an inning.
5. No, he would be dead.
6. It equals seventy.
7. You would have two.
8. Sixty minutes is the correct answer.
9. He would have nine sheep.
10. None; it was Noah.
11. There are twelve.

Well, how well did you do on the little quiz? How smart are you? Did you at least get half of them right? Did you say yes? Ah hah! Got ya! There is no half; there are eleven questions. Oops!

Did you know that it doesn't matter how smart you are, or how healthy you are, or how much you read your Bible? You cannot stop the inevitable appointed by God. It is already written in your life's book.

Have you ever thought deep and hard about the process of life? No self-definition will help you make sense of time or space or any reality you know apart from God. It doesn't matter about any of the things of the world, because in Him you move, in Him you live, and in Him you have your being. God created when you were born and created when you will die. He is the author of the Book of Life, and He knows it from cover to cover. But only God knows the whole story!

But this is not news to you. I'm sure you've been around a block or two, and you know what's up. You also know the world today is a pretty mixed-up, scary world. There are so many people who have guns nowadays and use them radically. There are also so many gangs everywhere, and they are out of control. People are committing crimes of all kinds and committing adultery, and people have just gone crazy.

But when you try to walk right with the Lord, you can be amongst all of this and be safer than those who don't care if they walk right and are in the middle of a Bible study. Think about how safe they are (Job 11:18). God gives you the ability to sleep regardless of the circumstances around you. In fact, God does not stop meeting our needs till we die. If we depend on God for all things, the outcome is always perfect. Even when it may not seem like our perfect, it's God's perfect.

Some Interesting Bible Facts

In the Old Testament times, people wore sackcloth to show they were in mourning.

The number of times *God* appears in the Bible is 3,358.

The number of times *Lord* appears in the Bible is 7,736.

The words *"don't be afraid"* appears in the Bible 365 times.

The first three words in the Bible are "In the beginning."

The very last word in the Bible is "amen."

The seven archangels are Michael, Gabriel, Raphael, Uriel, Chamuel, Jophiel, and Zadkiel.

Moses was four months old when Pharaoh's daughter found him in a basket.

The seven deadly sins are lust, pride, anger, greed, envy, sloth, and gluttony.

The two men in the Bible who never died are Enoch and Elijah. God took them to heaven.

When I am down, I look to Jesus to pick me up, and when I need some strength and when I have questions, He has all the right answers. God can fix any spiritual, emotional, physical, directional, or eternal situation. God is sufficient enough, and if you try to figure these things out on your own, you will fail. I know I have tried so many times to try to figure it all out, but whom am I fooling but myself? I have no clue and never will. I am so powerless that my weakness empowers me to trust the power that prevails. It may not be today and it may not be tomorrow, but one of these days, without that trust, one day you will lie down and the only way to get up will be to ask God, and then He will ask you, "Am I sufficient enough now?" And that's when you will be asking for His mercy on you. Wise up, my friend! Here's a question for you: is the Lord your shepherd?

Love Never Fails
>Love is patient, love is kind,
>Through Jesus Christ, love you will find.
>Love does not envy, it is not puffed up,
>Seek Him with all your heart, He will fill your cup.
>Love does not behave rudely, does not seek its own,
>Be kind to others, for this God has shown.
>Love believes, and hope endures all things,
>Give love to all for blessings God brings.

My dad served in the U.S. Navy during World War II. He was a very patriotic man. He loved to fly his American flag at home on the flagpole on the front porch. I can remember that when we were kids, Mom and Dad would take us to our town parade, and my dad would make us kids stand up at any American flag that would pass. We had to put our hand over our heart, and my dad always removed his hat until the flag passed us. This was a must if you went with my dad. I didn't like it so much then, but as I got older, I started to understand the importance of the support for the flag and what it represents. Here is a poem I came across that my dad wrote.

Our American Heritage
Written by Herbert Leon Hatcher, 1956

>As we labor and sweat on this earthly soil, let us never forget for whom we toil.
>And as the long days turn into short years, let us never regret all the blood, sweat, and tears.
>And as we look back on the pages of time, life is just a short verse of God's book divine.

Now as we grow older and hair starts to gray, God's
meaning is clear why we should pray.
By His grace and divine power, He put faith in us, and
gave us this land with a full deed of trust.
As His chosen people we would do what He asked, to
make this land great, a nation, was our task.
Our forefathers cleared timber from off of the land, to
grow food for families with God's helping hand.
We rolled up our sleeves and hitched up the plow, and
started the sweat rolling from off our brow.
God gave us this country and I'm sure it's the best, for
many times now it's been put to His test.
We've had hard times, famine, flood, and drought, and
many a storm that has hit with a clout.
There've been battles and wars in our two hundred years,
which caused most families to shed many tears.
But now we are stronger and grow day by day, thank God
for the wisdom of learning to pray.
We still will have problems throughout this great land, but
we can face it with strength and God's helping hand.
There is crime in the streets and much family strife, but
God didn't say it would be a trouble-free life.
We all know it hasn't been peaches and cream, but what
we have in America is other nations' dream.
I speak of the freedom as Americans we share God's gift
we take for granted with nary a care.
We should mourn for other nations as I'm sure God
does too, and pray that their leader will be a leader
that's true.
There're warlords, dictators, monarchs, and kings, who
are not for the common man, or so sometimes it seems.

They lay up treasures for themselves but not in the house
  of God, not so the common Shepherd with His staff
  and His rod.
It certainly is grand all the freedom we share,
  as American citizens we have them without care.
As we grow older and become more racially mixed,
  we should remember to thank God for seventeen
  seventy-six.
We were given our freedom to become a great land,
  to have religious and civil liberty with God's
  helping hand.

Now as we grow older and wiser with age, thank God for all
things, especially *our American heritage.*

If you are struggling to believe in yourself, please don't forget
that Jesus believes in you; and if He believes in you, you
have every reason in the world to believe in you too.

We are created for purpose. We're created for dreams, but
none of these things can take place if we don't believe in ourselves. God gave me the ability to write this book, but it was
up to me to put my emotions and my actions behind it. God
wasn't going to do it for me. I find that the more I pray about
something, the more my concerns become aligned with the
Lord's concerns. From the day we were created, the Lord's
hand has been on us, guiding us and holding us fast. If we
look at the verses in Psalm 139, we can see several scriptures that tell us the Lord wants us to be successful.

I am going to go the extra mile and put my whole heart and soul into this book so I can confidently say in a humble way that I tried my hardest and did my best to glorify my King and all the power He brings. It didn't come easy and it didn't come overnight, but I had to be smart and refuse to give up. I also had to believe that success could be mine.

God yearns for His children to succeed in life, but not the success to be wealthy, as you can buy the most beautiful house in the world, but that doesn't make it a home. The type of success I am talking about is more than just financial victory or power or fame. It involves a balance of achievement both professionally and personally, a wholesomeness that occurs only when we are pursuing our God-given purpose and not our own selfish ambitions. This stuff can be a little heavy at times. "But I press on to take hold of that for which Jesus took hold of me" (Philippians 3:12–14).

Please read this carefully. I am not trying to discourage you from God's power or His control or influence in your life. But too many Christians settle for, "If it's meant to be, then it will happen." They sit back and wonder why God doesn't send down little notes from heaven with answers to all of their questions or dreams. Sure, it's possible, but I don't believe God uses that method for most of us. He wants us to grow and develop. He wants to see us mature and learn through the experiences He gives us.

He wants us to be confident and positive individuals. If you had to choose between two people to represent you, whom would you prefer? Someone who is a whiner and keeps waiting for something good to happen, or someone who is a warrior, confident and poised, and brings with them an attitude of optimism that touches everything they do? I would choose the second one, and I believe that's what God wants. He doesn't want negative. John Maxwell writes in his book called, "Make Today Count" "that a dream without a positive attitude produces a daydreamer". "A positive attitude without a dream produces a pleasant person who can't progress". "A dream together with a positive attitude produces a person with unlimited possibilities and potential".

The Lord's Love and Protection

The Lord's love and protection are never so far,
That He cannot reach us wherever we are.
His arm outstretched like an eagle's wing,
Hovering with the love and care He brings.
Enlightened by His comforting power,
We may rest and be assured every day, every hour.

COURAGE Brown-Bag Burrito

Ingredients:
  1 pound lean ground beef
  1 can (16 ounces) refried beans
  ⅔ cup enchilada sauce
  ¼ cup water
  3 tablespoons minced onion
  1½ tablespoons chili powder
  1½ teaspoons garlic powder
  ¾ teaspoon salt
  ½ teaspoon dried oregano
  15 to 20 flour tortillas (7 inches)
  1½ to 2½ cups shredded cheddar cheese

Directions:

In a large skillet brown ground beef; drain. Add next eight ingredients. Bring to a boil, and then reduce heat. Cover and simmer for 20 minutes.

Heat 3–4 tortillas in the microwave until warm, about 45 seconds. Spoon 3–4 tablespoons of meat with a pinch of cheese onto each tortilla. Roll up. Wrap each burrito in a paper towel, then in foil. Repeat with remaining ingredients.

Serves 15–20.

A Daily Prayer for Protection

Lord God, I pray for Your protection as I begin this day. You are my hiding place, and under Your wings I can always find refuge. Protect me from trouble wherever I go, and keep evil far from me. No matter where I am, I will look to You as my protector, the one who fights for me every day. Your love and faithfulness, along with Your goodness and mercy, surround me. My trust is in You, God, and I give thanks to You for Your love and protection. In Jesus' name, amen.

"Where two or three come together in my name, there am I with them" (Matthew 18:20).

"For I know the plans I have for you," declares the Lord, "plans to prosper you and not to harm you, plans to give you hope and a future" (Jeremiah 29:11).

Jesus says, "I have come that they may have life, and that they may have it more abundantly" (John 10:10).

Here is another God-send I experienced. It is so amazing when God winks at you!

What I Always Knew, but Now I Know #4

One day I was on my hour lunch break, which consisted of me eating my lunch, reading my Bible for twenty minutes, and kicking my seat back and taking a fifteen-minute catnap before going back to work. On this day I did just that, but for some reason, I must have been really tired, because I was sleeping very well. All of a sudden there was the hardest, loudest knock on my window. It was so loud that I sat up in my seat very startled and with my heart pounding. I looked out my window expecting to see someone standing there, but there was no one there. *What? Where did they go so fast?*

I knew I had heard the knock; that's what had woken me up. I turned in my seat, looking all around my car, looking for someone. I even got out of my car and looked all around it and underneath it, but to my amazement, there was not a soul in sight—absolutely no one. *What? How is that?*

I got back into the car and looked down at my watch, and I couldn't believe it. I had exactly five minutes to get back to work. Had I not heard the hard knock, I would have been late going back. God, I know that was You. It had to be. Thank You! Awesome, isn't it? The most awesome thing about it for me is that the creator of the universe knew what I needed at that very moment. That just amazes me!

Did you know there's a two-word phrase listed in all sixty-six books of the Bible and that phrase is *fear not*? God doesn't want us to be afraid; He wants us to reach out and grab hold of life, the abundant life, with both hands. In Psalm 38:4, we read, "Taste and see that the Lord is good."

This is the most frequently repeated instruction, to fear not. He wants us to be strong and courageous. You can trust me. Fear not.

Why does God command us not to fear? Fear doesn't seem like the most serious vice in the world. It never made the list of seven deadly sins. No one ever received church discipline for being afraid. So why does God tell us to stop being afraid more often than He tells us anything else? My hunch is that the reason God says "fear not" so often is because we are tempted to avoid doing what God asks us to do.

What I Always Knew, but Now I Know #5

I had been praying this particular week or two about a situation I desperately needed answers for. I prayed and I prayed, and about two weeks later, I received a text on my cell phone that read, "Teresa, if you believe, you can achieve." That was all it said. What? Who would send me this text? After all, it had to be someone who knew me; it had my name in it.

I looked at the number, thinking, *Who would tell me something like that?* It matched so well to what I had been praying about. Who would know what I needed to hear? I had never talked to anyone about my prayer, so where had this come from? I checked out the number and tried to call it back to see who this was, but the number was not a good number. It kept giving me the recording, "You have reached a number that is no longer in service." Well then, what the heck, so I tried to look up on the computer to see if there was any name attached to that number, but no such number was found.

I then looked at the text again, and I couldn't believe my eyes. It just happened to be the seventh text of seventy-seven. Talk about an intervention! Oh my, if that wasn't, I don't know what is. Only God knew my prayer, and when I really stopped and gave it some thought, I knew it was God. As bizarre as it seemed, I knew in my heart that it was the answer to my prayer. I am still amazed by that one. I know He knows my name, but to have it actually said to me, "Oh my!" is all I can say. God is so good and so amazing.

I don't know why I have been so blessed to have experienced these things, but I am honored and grateful and so very thankful that the God I love loves me so very much and takes the time to show me. Wow! Wow! Wow!

A Prayer for Good Health

We bless You, Lord. You are our Jehovah, the healer of our diseases. Our bodies are the temple of Your Spirit, so we pray for protection from that which could bring harm to us physically. Guard us from stresses that steal our emotional strength and lower our immunity to fight infection. Heal us of past traumas that may affect our present or future health. Teach us how to discipline our bodies so we can grow stronger and increase our physical stamina. When challenges arise, we need not fear, for You have given us a spirit of power, of love, and of a sound mind.

As the Great Physician, You know us so well. You ordained every part of our bodies even before we were born. Help us to treat our bodies with respect as Your beloved creations. We want to serve You with excellence and to fear no more the diseases that riddle the body and bring dangerous results. Safeguard us with wisdom to use well, the rest of our lives. Our health is in Your hands, Lord, and our trust and faith are in You. In Jesus' name, amen.

Finding your purpose can be challenging. I am absolutely convinced that each of us is created with a God-given purpose. It's what my life and yours are all about. Some people seem to know what their purpose is when they are just children, while some a little older. Some people just have a passion for the Lord in their heart that doesn't go away. They want to trust in God, and they are ready to see all their dreams come true.

For others, though, they don't want to see that their dreams can come true. They are in a dark, and empty place in their heart, but even if that is where you are, just look harder. It may take some time to see it, but that doesn't mean it isn't there. Since you have picked up this book, maybe something in here will click and help you to find your purpose, or maybe you're looking for an inspirational word that will hit home. Maybe you just wanted to see if others have experienced what you have experienced, and it helps to confirm what you already know, that there is a God and He is amazing. Whatever your search may be, just pray and ask God to help you find your purpose and to help you find your worth. You are worthy to accomplish when God is put first. Remember, you were created according to God's design and for His distinct pleasure. May your journey to find your purpose open your eyes, open your heart, and open the door to a whole new way of loving God.

I didn't really know I wanted to be a writer—well, not completely—but as I said earlier, I believe that God puts desires in our hearts through our dreams, through our passions, and through what brings us joy. When we look through all of those things, we can find our purpose as we discover the customized blueprint, the pattern God's made for each of us. It is my prayer for you that as you look to God for your purpose, you will continue along your journey by living creatively and with hope in the knowledge that God wants the best for you.

God's presence: "Never will I leave you; never will I forsake you" (Hebrews 13:5).

God's protection: "I am your shield, your very great reward" (Genesis 15:1).

God's power: "I will strengthen you" (Isaiah 41:10).

God's provision: "I will help you" (Isaiah 41:10).

God's leading: "He goes on ahead of them" (John 10:4).

God's purposes: "That I might show you My power and that My name might be proclaimed in all the earth" (Exodus 9:15–16).

God's cleansing: "If we confess our sins, He is faithful and just and will forgive us our sins and purify us from all unrighteousness" (1 John 1:9).

God's goodness: "No good thing does He withhold from those whose walk is blameless". (Psalm 84:11)

God's faithfulness: "For the sake of His great name, the Lord will not reject His people.

God's guidance: "He guides the humble" (Psalm 25:9).

God's wise plan: "We know that in all things God works for the good of those who love Him" (Romans 8:28).

Losing Life to Find the Soul

"Those of you who would save your life will lose it".

"Those of you who will lose your life for Me and the good news will save it".

"How does it help a person to gain the whole world and forfeit the soul"? (Matthew 16:25).

Child in His Arms

"Whoever welcomes a child in My name also welcomes Me. And whoever welcomes Me welcomes The one who sent me". (Mark 9:37)

Moving Mountains

"If you tell this mountain, rise and leap into the sea, and have no doubt in your heart, but believe that what is said will happen, It will be yours. So I say to you, all that you pray and ask for, Believe you have received it and it will be yours. When you stand praying, if you hold something against someone, Forgive, so your Father will also forgive your wrong steps". (Mark 11:23–25)

On the Mount of Olives

"Beware that no one leads you astray. Many will come in my name, saying, "I am," and they will lead many astray. But when you hear of wars and rumors of wars, do not be frightened; these things must occur. But the end is not yet; nations will rise against nations, Kingdoms against kingdoms, and earthquakes in the lands, And there will be famines. These things are the beginning of the last agonies". (Mark 13:5–8)

Sermon on the Mount

"Blessed are the poor in spirit, for theirs is the kingdom of heaven".

"Blessed are they who mourn, for they will be comforted".

"Blessed are the gentle, for they will inherit the earth".

"Blessed are the hungry and thirsty for justice, for they will be heartily fed".

"Blessed are the merciful, for they will obtain mercy".

"Blessed are the clean in heart, for they will see God".

"Blessed are the peacemakers, for they will be called the children of God".

"Blessed are they who are persecuted for the sake of justice, for theirs is the kingdom of heaven".

"Blessed are you when they revile, persecute, and speak evil and lie because of Me".

"Rejoice and be glad, for your reward in the heavens is huge". (Matthew 5:3–12)

The Lord's Prayer

"Our Father who art in heaven, hallowed be Your name your kingdom come, Your will be done, on earth as it is in heaven. Give us this day our daily bread, and forgive our debts as we have forgiven our debtors, and lead us not into temptation, but deliver us from evil, For yours is the kingdom, the power, and the glory forever." (Matthew 6:9–13)

Sometimes Love Hurts

Tactful correction is one of the most difficult parts of friendship;
Find fault with the behavior, not the person.

Friends Strengthen Us

Two people are better off than one, for they can help each other succeed. If one person falls, the other can reach out and help. But someone who falls alone is in real trouble. Likewise, two people lying close together can keep each other warm. But how can one be warm alone? A person standing alone can be attacked and defeated, but two can stand back to back and conquer. "Three are even better, for a triple-braided cord is not easily broken" (Ecclesiastes 4:9–12).

What I Always Knew, but Now I Know #6

I have a best friend named Joy. Joy is one of the best friends I have ever had. We have been friends since high school, about forty years now. We also have nicknames for each other; she calls me Myrt and I call her Mona. She says I'm slow like a turtle, so she calls me Myrtle the turtle. I don't think I am. She moans about everything, so I named her Mona the moaner.

Joy believed in Jesus, but she did not like to go to church and hadn't been since she was a little girl. I loved to go to church as often as I could. I would ask her to go with me all the time, and she would always say the same thing: "No, I don't like church," and I would say, "Come on, Joy. Just go with me; you might like it." Her answer was always the same: "Nope." Over and over again I would ask her. For about ten years this went on, with still the same answer—"Nope!"

Finally, I learned—gee, it only took ten years to let go and let God—so I just started praying about it. I prayed that the Lord would soften her heart and put a desire in her heart to want to go to church. I prayed and prayed. Then one day I asked Joy again to go to church and again she said no. I asked her, "Joy are we best friends?" and she said, "Yes. Why?" I said, "Would you please, for your best friend, go to church with me just once? If you go just once, I won't ever ask you to go again. I promise!"

I couldn't believe my ears, when she said yes. What? I had to ask her to repeat it. "What? You will?"

She said yes but loudly emphasized, "Just once, Myrtle, just once."

I told her, "No problem." Grinning as big as I could, I said quietly, "Thank You, Jesus, You answered my prayer of softening her heart to say yes she would go". I then started praying and praying that the sermon that day would be the perfect sermon for her and that maybe it would give her a desire to come back. That was my prayer. God is so wonderful; He answered yet another prayer. The sermon was absolutely perfect and, in fact, couldn't have been more perfect.

Joy went down front and gave her life to Jesus that day. I was bawling like a baby. I got to witness another miracle before my very eyes—the miracle that would change her life and mine forever. I am so grateful and thankful for God's grace, for His unending love and perfection. The whole thing was absolutely beautiful, and what was even more beautiful about it was the fact that it was in God's timing and it was perfect. He just knows what we need when we need it. Nobody but God could have handled that the way He did with such perfection.

Joy has now become a member of the church, serves every Sunday in the coffee ministry, and has since brought her husband, her daughter, a son, a few grandkids, as well as a few of her cousins. She is a full-fledged churchgoer now and loves it. She tries really hard not to miss a service. She has even attended a few Bible studies. Glory and praise be to God—You are amazing!

You are such a patient God. You knew just the right time and perfected it. Thank You.

Thank You, Jesus, for the wonderful memories You so graciously give us. Please, I ask You, don't let me get so busy that I forget to thank You, God. You are busy all the time, and You never forget me.

Slow down and enjoy God's grace. Don't mistake pride for independence; sometimes the best thing to do is to humble yourself and ask God for help. When you are faced with a decision, going to God is a first option, not a last resort. Anytime we don't keep God first, life gets messy and can take ten years to accomplish something, and we tend to get stressed out. With God's help, we can move from dependence on self to dependence on God.

Every time you receive what some call an unexplainable event, it's a direct and personal message of reassurance from God to you, what I call a God-send. It's similar to when you were a kid sitting at the dining room table and you looked up and saw Mom or Dad give you that wink. You had a nice feeling from that small, silent communication. What did it mean? Probably something like, "Hey, kid, I'm proud of you, and everything is going to be alright." That's what a God-send is. So every time you think it's a coincidence, it's not. It's God's way of giving you His small, silent communication. Sometimes I just look up, smile, and say," I know that was You, God Thanks!"

Dear God, thank You for helping me to realize that "not I, but Christ" is not just a catchphrase contained in the Bible, but it is a way of living that allows Christ to have first place in my life. Help me to not live only for myself, but also give me the grace to live for You and to bring glory to Your name. In Jesus' name, amen.

What is your purpose in life? Theologians have debated and discussed this question for centuries. The short answer to this question is simply this: our purpose in life—are you ready?—is to bring glory to God! You were created by God to bring glory to God by living for God. That is a simple answer to a difficult question. The real trick, though, is to understand that your life is not your life. You have been bought with a price.

When Jesus died on the cross, He paid the penalty for all your sins and for the sins of the world. Through His death on the cross, it is now possible to live for God with reckless abandon. Living for God with reckless abandon is not a motto or a catchphrase either; it is a passionate pursuit of your desires to His desires. "Not I, but Christ" simply summarizes the desires of a person whose heart and mind and will have been captured by another. For the person who makes this declaration, their direction is no longer living for themselves, but living for and longing for the day when he or she will hear from the Savior, "Well done, my good and faithful servant" (Matthew 25:21).

Dear God, thank You for giving the greatest gift ever given to man. Help me to keep this priceless treasure in my heart. Help me to share Jesus with my family and my friends. Give me the wisdom and courage to share Jesus without fear. In Jesus' name, amen.

Place your trust in His promise to save you. If you confess with your mouth that Jesus is Lord and believe in your heart that God raised Him from the dead, you will be saved. For it is believing in your heart that you are made right with God, and it is by confessing with your mouth that you are saved. As the Scriptures tell us, "Anyone who trusts in him will never be disgraced" (Romans 10:9).

HOLY Basil Olive Dip

Basil olive dip; serve with bread loaf

Ingredients:

½ cup olive oil
½ cup fresh basil leaves
1 tablespoon garlic salt
1 tablespoon parmesan cheese
½ teaspoon salt
½ teaspoon pepper
1 loaf fresh bread
Optional: ¼ teaspoon of red pepper flakes

Directions:

Chop basil finely.

Gently mix basil, garlic salt, parmesan cheese, salt, pepper, and red pepper flakes.

49

Add olive oil.

Serve olive oil dip and fresh bread as an appetizer or with meals.

Makes ¾ cup of olive oil dip.

A HELPFUL HINT

Helps get rid of rash, fungus, acne, eczema

In a cast iron skillet *only*, on medium heat, brown 2 cups of flour (any kind).

Toss and turn flour in skillet until brown.

Let cool, and then put it in a container.

Apply like powder.

A HELPFUL HINT

Helps get rid of headaches, mild to severe

Take a banana; eat it.

Use the banana peel from the inside and lay it on your forehead.

Apply a very warm washcloth or small hand towel over the top of the banana peel.

Leave on forehead for 30–45 minutes.

** A HELPFUL HINT**

Helps pets get rid of constipation

Take anything with pumpkin in it.

Give your dog about a quarter of a cup for two days.

Will help dog's bowels and digestive system.

** A HELPFUL HINT**

Helps with foot dryness (athlete's foot)

Take a small onion, white or brown, and cut the onion into thin slices.

Take a slice of bread, and cut it into strips about an inch long.

Between each toe where there is dryness or fungus, put a piece of onion next to a piece of bread.

Use an Ace bandage to hold in place, and then put on a sock.

If fungus is on the bottom of your foot, apply onion and bread flat on foot and apply an Ace bandage. To hold it in place, put on a sock and leave overnight.

Remove and repeat a couple of days if needed.

Wash area the next day and dry completely.

Fungus will soon be gone.

———————————◆———————————

When we go and apply for a job, we always want to say just the right things, and we try to wear the right clothes and have a resume that makes us shine with the perfect description of our work history. Then we sit back and hope we're the perfect candidate for the job.

Read the qualifications of this applicant and let me know if you think he's fit for the job. Time is crucial. Will he qualify for the position in your heart?

Address: Ephesians 1:20

Phone: Romans 10:13

Website: The Bible

Keywords: Jesus Christ, Lord and Savior

My name is Jesus, the Christ. Many call Me "Lord." I have sent you My resume because I'm seeking the top management position in your heart. Please consider My accomplishments as set forth in My resume.

Qualifications

"I founded the earth and established the heavens" (Proverbs 3:19).

"formed man from the dust of the ground" (Genesis 2:7).

"I breathed into man the breath of life" (Genesis 2:7).

"The blessings of the Abrahamic covenant come upon your life through Me" (Galatians 3:14).

Occupational Background

*I've only had one employer (Luke 2:49).

*I've never been tardy, absent, disobedient, slothful, or disrespectful.

"My employer has nothing but rave reviews for Me" (Matthew 3:15–17).

Skills and Work Experience

*Some of My skills and work experience include empowering the poor to be poor no more, healing the sick, restoring sight to the blind, and setting at liberty those that are bruised (Luke 4:18).

"I am a wonderful counselor" (Isaiah 9:6). "People who listen to Me shall dwell safely and shall not fear evil" (Proverbs 1:33).

"Most importantly, I have the authority, ability, and power to cleanse you of your sins" (John 1:7–9).

Educational Background

"I encompass the entire length of knowledge, wisdom, and understanding" (Proverbs 2:6).

"In Me are hidden all the treasures of wisdom and knowledge" (Colossians 2:3).

"My Word is so powerful, it has been described as being a lamp unto your feet and a light unto your path" (Psalms 119:105).

"I can even tell you all of the secrets of your heart" (Psalm 44:21).

Major Accomplishments

"I was an active participant in the greatest summit meeting of all time" (Genesis 1:26).

"I laid down My life so that you may live" (2 Corinthians 5:15).

"I defeated the archenemy of God and mankind and made a show of them openly" (Colossians 2:15).

*I've miraculously fed the poor, healed the sick, and raised the dead, and there are many more major accomplishments, too many to mention here. You can read them on My website, which is located at www. the BIBLE. You don't need an Internet connection or computer to access My website.

References

*Believers and followers worldwide will testify to My divine healings, salvation, deliverance, miracles, restoration, and supernatural guidance.

Now that you have read My resume, I'm confident I am the only candidate qualified to fill the position in your heart. I will direct your paths and lead you into everlasting life. When can I start? Time is of the essence.

I don't know if it's just me, or if you do this as well, but I thank Jesus for so many things, big or small, happy or sad. I find myself thanking Him for a parking spot, for my food, for my beautiful family, and for my health even when I hurt. I find myself getting emotional quite often when I think of all my blessings and how loving and kind God is to give me all that He gives me: love, grace, empathy, support, understanding, friendship, forgiveness, and a good spanking when I need it. He is the ultimate loving Father, and *He loves me*! I am in awe of Him now and forevermore.

Here are a few poems for you.

I Am a Christian
> When I say, "I am a Christian,"
> I'm not shouting, "I am saved."
> I'm whispering, "I get lost,"
> That is why I chose this way.
> When I say, "I am a Christian,"
> I don't speak of it with pride.
> I'm confessin that I stumble,
> And I need someone to be my guide.
> When I say, "I am a Christian,"
> I'm not trying to be strong.

I'm professing that I am weak
And pray for strength to carry on.
When I say, "I am a Christian,"
I'm not bragging of success.
My flaws are too visible,
But God believes I'm worth it.
When I say, "I am a Christian,"
I still feel the sting of pain.
I have my share of heartaches,
Which is why I seek His name.
When I say, "I am a Christian,"
I do not wish to judge.
I have no authority,
I only know I'm loved.

Recipe for a House of Love

A home made from love
Is what God intends,
Filled with all of our family,
Love is not blind nor pretends.
The recipe is simple,
The ingredients are clear,
Keeping God close is essential
For love to be near.
Start with some laughter,
Don't forget to pray,
Mix a few smiles,
And God will make clear the way.

The Journey

Life is but a stopping place, a pause in what's to be,
A resting place along the road to sweet eternity.
We all have different journeys, different paths along the way,

We all were meant to learn some things, but never
meant to stay.
Our destination is a place far greater than we know,
For some the journey is quicker, for some the journey is slow.
And when the journey finally ends, we'll claim a
great reward,
And find an everlasting peace together with the Lord.

Letting Go Can Be Easy, or It Can Be Hard

To let go does not mean to stop caring; it means I can't
do it for someone else.
To let go is not to cut myself off; it's the realization I can't
control another.
To let go is not to enable, but to allow learning from nat-
ural consequences.
To let go is to admit powerlessness, which means the out-
come is not in my hands.
To let go is not to try to change or blame another; it's to
make the most of myself.
To let go is not to care for, but to care about.
To let go is not to fix, but to be supportive.
To let go is not to judge, but to allow another to be a
human being.
To let go is not to try arranging the outcomes, but to allow
others to effect their own destinies.
To let go is not to be protective; it's to permit another to
face reality.
To let go is not to deny, but to accept.
To let go is not to nag, scold, or argue; instead, search
your shortcomings and correct them.
To let go is not to adjust everything to my desire, but to
take each day as it is and cherish it.

To let go is not to criticize myself, but to try and become
what I dream I can be.
To let go is not to regret the past, but to grow and live for
the future.

"Let all bitterness and wrath and clamor and slander
be put away from you, along with all malice". "Be kind
to one another, tenderhearted, forgiving one another,
as God in Christ forgave you" (Ephesians 4:31–32).

When the apostle Paul wrote that we are to let go of all bitterness, wrath, anger, clamor, and slander, he was saying
that we must make the first move. We must be intentional in
letting all of these sinful behaviors go and take the initiative to
be kind to others, showing tender hearts and remembering to
forgive others. Especially considering how much more we've
been forgiven, our forgiving others is infinitely more on the
scale of how much God has forgiven us in Christ.

One way to let go is to be looking forward. You can't be
looking forward and backward at the same time. "Forgetting
what lies behind us" doesn't mean we can erase it from our
memories. We can't do that, but that's okay. That's how we
learn; mistakes are great teachers. But Paul is telling us to
forget about it and move on. Stop dwelling on the past. Don't
trip over what's behind you. Press forward, not backward,
Press ahead—the goal in front of you, not behind you. That
prize seems closer today than it did last year, doesn't it?
Keep pressing forward.

"Brothers, I do not consider that I have made it my own. But one thing I do, forgetting what lies behind and straining forward to what lies ahead, I press on toward the goal for the prize of the upward call of God in Christ Jesus" (Philippians 3:13–14).

"Remember not the former things nor consider the things of old. Behold, I am doing a new thing; now it springs forth, do you not perceive it? I will make a way in the wilderness and rivers in the desert" (Isaiah 43:18–19).

FAITHFUL Fish Tacos

Ingredients:

1 pound fresh or frozen fish (tilapia, swai, red snapper, or whatever kind you desire)
2 tablespoons taco seasoning
2 tablespoon olive oil
Directions:
Pat fish dry with paper towels.
Cut into fillets 1 inch wide and 5 inches long.
Mix 2 tablespoons of your favorite taco seasoning.
Mix 2 tablespoons of olive oil.
Coat fish on both sides.
Place on aluminum foil on the grill.
Cook approximately 4–5 minutes on medium heat.
Fish should be moist and flaky.

Serve with tortillas.

Have you ever in your life thought that Jesus could be as amazing as He is? Did you ever think He could love you as much as He does? Have you ever thought about how many people there are in this universe and that He knows *you* intimately? Did you ever think that love could be so beautiful and perfect and last forever if you choose it? Have you ever just sat back and thought about how blessed you are in your own special way? All these things are for each of us. But the ultimate gift is the gift of salvation for eternity, and it is *free, free indeed.*

I said, "I will watch my ways and keep my tongue from sin; I will put a muzzle on my mouth while in the presence of the wicked." "So I remained utterly silent, not even saying anything good." "But my anguish increased; my heart grew hot within me. While I meditated, the fire burned; then I spoke with my tongue: "Show me, Lord, my life's end and the number of my days: let me know how fleeting my life is. You have made my days a mere handbreadth; the span of my years is as nothing before You. Everyone is but a breath, even those who seem secure." (Psalm 39:1-13)

"Surely everyone goes around like a mere phantom; in vain they rush about, heaping up wealth without knowing whose it will finally be." (Psalm 39:6).

"Therefore we do not lose heart. Though outwardly we are wasting away, yet inwardly we are being renewed day by day" (2 Corinthians 4:16).

"For I know the plans I have for you," declares the Lord, "plans for welfare and not for evil, to give you a future and a hope. Then you will call upon Me and come and pray to Me, and I will hear you" (Jeremiah 29:11–12).

"Keep your life free from the love of money. Be content with what you have, for He has said, "I will never leave you nor forsake you" (Hebrews 13:5).

"Teaching them to observe all that I have commanded you. And behold, I am with you always, to the end of the age" (Matthew 28:20)._

A HELPFUL HINT

Helps fight stains

   Hydrogen peroxide (2 ounces)
   Dawn dishwashing soap (1–1½ ounces)
   Baking soda (2 tablespoons)

Directions:

   Add all ingredients; shake well.
   Saturate stain with mixture.
   Let dry and then vacuum.

I want to share an amazing letter with you. If for any reason you are struggling with love for the Lord or wonder if He loves you, you may have a different feeling in your heart after reading this letter. (This letter was created by putting scriptures together).

God's Love Letter to You

My child,
You may not know Me, but I know everything about you. I know when you sit down and when you rise up. I am familiar with all your ways; even the very hairs on your head are numbered.

You were made in My image. In Me you live and move and have your being.

You are My offspring. I knew you even before you were conceived. I chose you when I planned creation. You are not a mistake, for all your days are written in My book. I determined the exact time of your birth and where you would live. You are fearfully and wonderfully made. I knit you together in your mother's womb and brought you forth on the day you were born.

I have been misrepresented by those who don't know Me. I am not too distant and angry, but I am the complete expression of love. It is My desire to lavish My love on you, simply because you are My child and I am your Father. I offer you more than your earthly father ever could, for I am the perfect Father. Every good gift you receive comes from My hand, for I am your provider and I meet all of your needs. My plan for your future has always been filled with hope, because I love you with an everlasting love. My thoughts toward you are as countless as the sand on the seashore, and I rejoice over you with singing. I will never stop doing good for you, for you are My treasured possession.

I desire to establish you with all My heart and soul, and I want to show you great and marvelous things.

If you seek Me with all your heart, you will find Me. Delight in Me and I will give you the desires of your heart. It is I who gave you these desires, and I am able to do more for you than you can possibly imagine.

I am your greatest encourager, and I am also your Father who comforts you in all your troubles. When you are brokenhearted, I am close to you. As a shepherd carries a lamb, I have carried you close to My heart. One day I will wipe away every tear from your eyes, and I will take away all the pain you have suffered on earth. I am your Father, and I love you as I love My Son Jesus.

In Jesus My love for you is revealed; He is the exact representation of My being. He came to demonstrate that I am for you, not against you, and to tell you I am not counting your sins. Jesus died so that you and I could be reconciled. His death was the ultimate expression of My love for you. I gave up everything I love that I might gain your love. If you receive the gift of My Son Jesus, you receive Me, and nothing will ever separate you from My love again.

Come home and I will throw the biggest party heaven has ever seen. I have always been Father and will always be Father. My question is, Will you be My child? I am waiting for you.

Love, Your dad, almighty God

I would like to share another God-send. His timing is always so perfect.

What I Always Knew, but Now I Know #7

I love going to church, and I am blessed with it being right down the street from my house. I have been attending this church for about nine to ten years now. The services are awesome, the people are nice, and the coffee and muffins are so yummy. I love to sit in my certain little area; I don't know why, but I do. I greet and meet new people every week.

I recently met a new friend, Renee, who also sits in the area I do. Week after week we greeted each other, but on this one particular day, we somehow connected beyond a "Hello. How are you?" We are now good friends. I love Renee. She is a kind person and is as beautiful on the inside as she is on the outside, just a kind and gentle spirit and a God-fearing soul.

We have many things in common, but our most important common thing is our love for our Lord Jesus Christ. Renee and I love to pray, and we pray about all kinds of things, but at the top of the list at this time is prayer for my daughter Lacey, who is battling leukemia. The Lord is still so gracious in this battle and shows us His love in Lacey's results. Renee and I are always talking about how wonderful and merciful the good Lord is, and that His timing is remarkable.

We also found out that not only are we sisters in Christ, but we are neighbors and live right down the way from each other. We were jazzed, that out of all the people at the church, we were neighbors in the same mobile home park. I nick-named her my SAF, which stands for "sister and friend."

One Sunday after church, Renee and I were texting back and forth and again praising God and His mighty power. I made a comment to her, "Yes, He is awesome. I'm sticking to His team. Jesus always wins."

The following Sunday my daughter Lacey called me and told me she had something for me. She said, "Mom, it was so you"! "I thought of you as soon as I saw it."

I asked her, "What is it? Tell me. I love surprises, but I want to know now!" Smile!

She said, "You have to come down and get it."

I said, "Okay, I will be right there." So I got there, walked in, and she handed me a T-shirt. I couldn't believe my eyes. With my eyes as big as they could go and with my mouth open as wide as it would stretch, I had that look of shock. Written on the shirt, of all things it could have said, it read, "TEAM JESUS."

I about fell over. *What? No way! What? It says TEAM JESUS on it!* I couldn't believe my eyes, yet I could. I knew without a shadow of a doubt that this was yet another sign from my precious and gracious Father that He hears me and knows my needs. Wow! Wow! Wow! Amazing, isn't it? I couldn't wait to tell Renee what Lacey, of all people, had gotten for me and what it said. She cried like I did.

God is so good. He hears me and knows just what I need when I need it, and He knew I would understand what the shirt means. That's how He gave me His sign. I am honored and humbled that He took the time to show me yet another *what I already knew, but now I know.* Thank You, Jesus. Take the time, look up, and say, "Thank You, Jesus. I know that was You."

GUARDIAN Angel Food Cake

Ingredients:

> ¼ teaspoon salt
> 1¼ cups egg whites (about nine)
> 1½ cups sugar, divided
> 1 cup cake flour
> 1¼ teaspoons cream of tartar
> ⅓ cup warm water
> 1 teaspoon vanilla extract or any you like
> Directions:
> Preheat oven to 350 degrees.
> Combine in a large bowl:
> Egg whites
> Vanilla extract
> Water
> Cream of tartar

Combine in a large bowl:

> Sugar
> Salt
> Cake flour

Combine the dry ingredients with the first four ingredients. Using a mixer, slowly mix for approximately 2 minutes. Once you have reached medium peaks, carefully spoon mixture into an ungreased tube pan or Bundt pan.

Bake for 35 minutes. With wooden skewer or toothpick, check the inner and outer wall; the toothpick should come out dry.

Cool upside down on cooling rack for 35 minutes before removing.

Optional: Frost or serve with strawberries on top.

I Have a Friend Named Jesus
    I have a friend named Jesus, there's no other friend like He.
    I have a friend named Jesus, gave His life to set me free.
    I have a friend named Jesus, a perfect sinless man.
    I have a friend named Jesus, for me He has a plan.
    I have a friend named Jesus, on Him I can rely.
    I have a friend named Jesus, all my needs He will supply.

The Gift of Friendship
    Friendship is a priceless gift
    That cannot be bought or sold,
    But its value is far greater
    Than a mountain made of gold
    For gold is cold and lifeless
    It can neither see nor hear
    And in the time of trouble
    It is powerless to cheer
    It has no ears to listen

No heart to understand,
It cannot bring you comfort
Or reach out a helping hand
So when you ask God for a gift
Be thankful if he sends
Not diamond, pearls or riches,
But the love of real true friends

By Helen Steiner Rice

Friends Like Us

Friends like us rely upon one another,
To inspire and encourage, to support each other,
In following our dreams as far as they'll take us.
Friends like us are winners,
Not only because we believe in ourselves,
But because we believe in each other.

Friendship

Sometimes in life you find a special friend,
Someone who changes your life just by being a part of it.
There's a friendship that stays right in the heart,
And you don't know how it happened or where it got
   its start.
But the happiness it brings you always gives you a
   special lift,
And you realize that friendship is God's most precious gift.

Did you ever think about being a Christian and that no two
Christians will ever have to say good-bye forever, because
they will reunite in heaven for eternity? Nothing will be lost
that is done in obedience to God. The Christian on his knees
sees more than the philosopher on his tiptoes.

"Praise Him; He is your God, and you have seen with your own eyes the great and astounding things that He has done for you" (Deuteronomy 10:21).

"Praise the Lord who has given His people peace, as He promised He would" (1 Kings 8:56).

"The Lord is my strong defender; He is the one who has saved me. He is my God, and I will praise Him; my Father God, and I will sing about His greatness" (Exodus 15:2).

"Let us praise God for His glorious grace, for the free gift He gives us in His Son Jesus" (Ephesians 1:6).

I would like to share with you another God-send.

What I Always Knew, but Now I Know #8

W hen my children and I moved to Fairbanks, Alaska, in 2000, I experienced so many divine interventions it was almost unbelievable. Yet when you believe, it isn't so unbelievable. With God all things are possible.

I worked for my brother Curtis, who owned a few nightclubs. I worked the door taking the money and as female security—whatever that means! But on this particular day, I had an overwhelming feeling that someone was trying to take a cocktail outside. I had no clue who, but someone was,

so I warned the big security of my feelings.

I went up to a group that was standing by the door and told them that drinks were not allowed outside, and they assured me they knew and they were not taking them out. A couple of people left, and a few more were leaving when a feeling came over me that it was the person at the door and ready to leave who was concealing a drink in their jacket.

If drinks were to go outside, the club could be shut down by law. I confronted them, and again they denied having anything in their jacket, but I knew differently—I felt it. So here came security, the big guys, asking who had the drink. I told security, "That one has it." Security asked that person to open their jacket, and sure enough, there was a mixed drink in a glass getting ready to walk out the door. Security couldn't believe that I knew the person had a drink. They asked me how I knew and I said, "I don't know; something just told me." Smile! God, I know it was You or Your angels.

When you get a little sign, listen to it. It's a God-send!

A Smile
> A smile costs nothing but gives much.
> It enriches those who give it.
> It takes but a moment,
> But the memory of it sometimes lasts forever.
> None are so rich or mighty
> That he can get along without it,
> And none are so poor that he cannot be made richer by it.
> A smile creates happiness in the home,
> Promotes goodwill in business,
> And is the cornerstone of friendship.
> It can perk up the weary, bring cheer to the discouraged,
> Sunshine to the sad, and it's nature's best antidote
>   for trouble.
> Yet it can't be bought, begged, borrowed, or stolen,
> For it has no value to anyone
> Until it is given away.

When we think about finding balance, we often put our attention on everything and everyone else and forget about ourselves. But in order to take care of others, we have to take care of ourselves too. We can only give so much before we run dry. The person responsible for taking care of me is me. We don't often skip a meal because we haven't got the time, right? Yet when it comes to feeding ourselves emotionally or spiritually, we often fall short. We have to take care of ourselves, whether it's spending time in God's Word or spending time behind a closed bathroom door. Allowing ourselves time to recharge is important. Make a commitment to yourself to take care of *you*!

"Everything is possible for him who believes" (Mark 9:23).

"I tell you the truth, if you have faith as small as a mustard seed, you can say to this mountain, Move from here to there" and it will move. Nothing will be impossible for you (Matthew 17:20).

"Come to Me all you who are weary and burdened, and I will give you rest" (Matthew 11:28).

"For You created my innermost being; You knit me together in my mother's womb" (Psalm 139:13).

Here's a little story that I thought was so inspiring. It makes you think about the pace you're going through life. Are you the type of person that would stop to smell the roses, or are you the type that would say, "Yep, nice" and keep on walking? It's important to take time for God's wondrous beauty. You will grow to appreciate your life or life in general, and it will give you a whole new sense of being.

While driving through the mountains of North Carolina, returning from an appointment, I felt hurried, pressured by all the "important stuff" waiting back home for my attention. Spotting a car stopped in the road ahead of me, I braked behind it, fuming a little, wondering what the problem could be. Then I saw one of those huge, silent turtles crossing the road at an unbearably slow pace. Waiting for this creature to pass, I observed it casually at first, then with great and particular care, reflecting upon its movements and then upon my own.

Why was I racing through life at breakneck speed? I looked from the turtle to the sweep of mountains in the distance, to the rich colors of the trees. Rolling down the car window, I felt the breeze of autumn lift my hair, and I sniffed mountain laurel. In that moment of simple quiescence, I tasted the beauty of life. I felt God's contemplative peace enter my heart.

It's easy to operate under the illusion that what we are doing is so important that we cannot stop doing it. We think we cannot slow down, especially for something so trivial as a turtle. But that is exactly the sort of thing we must never be too busy for.

Stopping is a spiritual art. It is the refuge where we drink life in. Maybe next time *stop* and take the time to smell the roses and appreciate God's beauty.

We all must conform to the ways of Jesus, not Jesus conforming to us. Jesus does not change; we must change. God also doesn't like us questioning His authority or His power or His holiness. God is a jealous God, and He wants us to love only Him.

We are all sinners. If you didn't know that already, then you do now! Not only are we sinners, but there is no greater sinner than the other in God's eyes. A sinner is a sinner is a sinner. We have our laws that punish to the severity of the crime committed, but in God's eyes, a murderer is no better off than the man who lied. The only difference between the sin and the sinner is his heart. When we sin it most likely is done with little heart in the middle of it, but yet God still loves the sinners heart. The heart is what Jesus will judge— the heart, not the sin. If your heart does not love Him, there is no faith, and without faith there is no understanding, and without understanding there is no holiness, and without holiness there is no salvation, and without salvation … well, you die, and you will not have eternal life. Uh! I think I will continue to try to conform to the ways of Jesus. Momma didn't raise no dummy!

"So also Christ, having been offered once to bear the sins of men, shall appear a second time for salvation without reference to sin to those who eagerly await him" (Hebrews 9:28).

When God sees you coming before Him, He only lets you come into His presence because He sees you in the eyes of Jesus (Ephesians 2:18). This means He sees your heart, because Jesus should be your heart. If Jesus is your heart, He will take care of your soul.

If you are reading your Bible and doing your praying but things seem to make you feel more like a sinner, be happy. You know why? Because Jesus is getting more and more into your heart, and it's getting you more and more in tune with His song. You are feeling the conviction of spiritual development.

A Wing and a Prayer
Under the wing of an angel, we feel protected,
Through prayers to God, we feel connected.

Peace is said to be offered on the wings of a dove,
Prayers can bring peace along hope, faith, and love.
Wings of a jet plane provide steady flight,
I pray you remain steady and strong through this fight.
Butterflies have wings to fly playfully free,
And free from evil you will soon be.

The Words to Say I Love You

I was there, yet you did not see Me. The times that you did cry,

I wrapped you in My loving arms, and I wiped the tears from your eyes.

Every prayer I heard and answered, every cry for help I came,

I cast down all your enemies and brought them all to shame.

You are My beloved child, whom I set free,

I removed your chains of darkness, because you believed in Me.

I am in you and you in Me, none can take us apart,

Where are the words to express My love?

They are written in your heart.

HOPE Greek Grilled Catfish

Ingredients:

6–8 catfish fillets (6–8 ounces each)
Greek seasoning
4 ounces feta cheese, crumbled
1 tablespoon dried mint
2 tablespoons olive oil
Fresh mint leaves or parsley, optional

Cherry tomatoes, optional

Directions:

Heat oven to 350 degrees.

Season both sides of fish with Greek seasoning. Sprinkle each fillet with 1 tablespoon feta cheese and ½ teaspoon mint. Drizzle 1 teaspoon of olive oil over each fillet.

Roll up fillets and secure with toothpicks. Grill over medium heat for 20–25 minutes or until fish flakes easily with a fork. You can also bake fillets in a baking dish for 30–35 minutes.

Garnish with mint leaves, parsley, or cherry tomatoes if desired.

Serves 6–8.

What I Always Knew, but Now I Know #9

A couple of days before Thanksgiving, on November 22, 1996, it was a horrific day. It is a day I will never forget, a day that changed my family's life forever. One of my sisters, Darnell, was killed in an automobile accident in Nevada; she was forty-one years old. She was adopting a two-year-old boy named Joey, and the final court date was December 10.

It was a two-car accident. The lady who hit my sister had a heart attack, which caused her to lose control of her car, accelerate, and hit my sister at an estimated speed of 110 miles an hour as she was waiting for this lady at the stop sign. The lady passed away, and my sister was killed instantly. I had never experienced a death in my immediate family before, and it was a heartache, and pain in my gut that I can't explain. Our family was devastated. Although we knew about life, and death, it didn't seem to ease the pain we were feeling.

So, for Thanksgiving in 1996, we all loaded up and headed for Nevada to make funeral arrangements. I remember us stopping along the way at a restaurant to have a so-called Thanksgiving meal, which tasted so awful, especially with my gut in knots. This whole thing just didn't seem real. It was the worst Thanksgiving I have ever had. Although the rest of us were all together, we were missing *one*, my sister. The weird thing about this is that the lady who hit my sister was a mother of six children, and my sister was one of six children. Also, this lady and my sister knew each other we later found out. How ironic is that?

We finally got things set up for the funeral, and it was now the viewing day. I thought for sure that by the looks of the car, as smashed as it was, just a ball of metal, that my sister would be missing some kind of body part or something. I didn't want to know and I didn't want to see. I was assuming my sister was not all in one piece. I remember my mom saying to us, "We need to do this as a family. We need to view her together." I think what my mom was actually saying was that she was weak in the knees and needed our support. And rightly so— she was the momma.

We all went into the room to view my sister, and all thanks to my wonderful heavenly Father, she was in one piece. Not only that, but she had only one scratch on her thigh, about three inches long. That was it. Her injuries were all internal. God is so merciful.

As we were sitting there in a private viewing sanctuary room, all five of us and my mom, and dad, we started praying, and reminiscing in our minds about all the wonderful memories we were so blessed with. I was thinking to myself, *Lord I don't know how I will get through this, but I will be praying for Your help.* I felt my sister was so distant from us, and I had already begun to miss her so badly. Then all of a sudden, while I was looking at my sister, the most bizarre thing happened. It looked as if she was breathing. I could actually see the sheet going up and down. I couldn't believe what I was seeing; I knew in my heart and in reality that she was gone, but I saw the sheet moving.

Later that night, as crazy as it seems, I decided to tell one of my sisters what I had seen. I said, "I know this sounds crazy, and I know she is gone, but I promise I saw the sheet moving as if she were breathing."

My sister said, "You're not going to believe this, but I saw the same thing but didn't know how to explain it, and didn't want you to think I was nuts."

We then mentioned it to the rest of our siblings, and they all said the very same thing. We all knew that she was not breathing, but with the Lord all things are possible. I believe with all my heart that He showed us the sheet moving so that we would know she was not dead, but she was sleeping in another place and was just fine. That was our sign from God that it was going to be okay.

From that moment on, I was able to process the loss here on earth, but I am anxiously waiting for our reunion for eternity. Thank You, Jesus, for your merciful love wrapped around us.

My dad wrote this poem after my sister passed. It's beautiful. He had such a gift for writing poems.

In Loving Memory of Darnell Elaine Hatcher (Knapp)
December 31, 1955–November 22, 1996

> We think of you in silence
> And make no outward show,
> But what it meant to lose you
> Only your family will ever know.
> You wished no one a farewell
> And didn't have a chance to say good-bye,

You were gone before anyone knew it
And only God will ever know why.
You were a dedicated family member and wife
And soon to be a mother to Joe,
And why the good Lord took you suddenly
Is something only God will ever know.
To some you will soon be forgotten
To others you're a part of their past,
But to your family who loved you dearly
Your memory will forever last.
You will never be forgotten
And as God knows from above,
That as long as we breathe and live
That you will always be loved.

Your Family
June 8, 1997

"Lord, I want to be near you, near to your heart, Loving the light, and hating the dark. I want to be who you made me to be, I want to make you proud of what I do, because what I do, I do it for You. God, You're so good. In Jesus name, Amen

———————————————◆———————————————

As believers in Jesus, we are promised a new life covered under the protection of God and His angels, in which nothing can ever separate us from His love. We can rest easy knowing that no matter what hardship we face, God is our provider and protector. He sends His angels to watch over us and protect us from the harm of the world. These angels can give us peace so we can focus on knowing there is a bigger plan that God has chosen us for.

"We proclaim how good You are and all of the wonderful things You have done" (Psalm 75:1).

"Praise the Lord, all people on earth; praise His glory and might" (1 Corinthians 16:28).

"God is wise and powerful; praise Him forever and ever" (Daniel 2:20).

"Sing to the Lord, praise the Lord. He rescues the oppressed from the power of evil people" (Jeremiah 20:13).

What I Always Knew, but Now I Know #10

In 2000, the year of the millennium, we lived in a three-bedroom apartment in the heart of Fairbanks, Alaska. It was amazing to see a moose walk by our living room window, and we lived on the second floor. Moose tend to run around in Alaska like dogs roam around here in California.

Oh my gosh, I can remember the northern lights! I'm not sure if you've ever heard of them, but if you have, then you kind of have an idea of what you think they look like. You just can't imagine the neon colors they are, and the brightness, and the beauty of them—simply spectacular. I have also heard somewhere that what the lights are, are gases in the air. I'm no scientist, so I'm not sure about all that. I have also heard that because it's just gases in the air, if you get enough people together on a mountaintop and make enough vibration with noise, you can make them move. Hmm … I don't know about that one either, but it sure sounds amazing. Maybe I should do some research, right?

While we were in Alaska, we experienced some really crazy happenings. On one particular night, I was at work and the kids were home. It was about 8:00 p.m. when all of a sudden, my son called and told me they smelled burning marshmallows. I asked him, "Burning marshmallows?"

He said, "Yes, Mom, and it's strong." I told him to have his sister look outside and see where it might be coming from, and all of a sudden, he said, "Mom, the apartment is on fire!"

I said, "What!" I told him, "Hang up, and you and your sister get out. Get the dog and birds and you guys get out and call 911. I will be right home." Man, I started praying and asking the Lord to please let my kids get out and be okay. *Oh Lord, oh Lord!*

I never drove so fast in my life, trying to get home to my kids. When I got there, the fire department was there already with hoses stretched. I saw flames shooting out of what looked like our apartment. I was shaking and frantically looking for my kids through all the people and fire trucks, and I finally saw them standing outside. It was snowing like heck, and it was about twenty-eight degrees. Yikes! I was never so relieved to see their faces. Thank You, Jesus.

Okay, so I saw the dog, but no birds. I gave my kids the biggest hugs, and we all started crying that all of us were all right. I asked the kids where the birds were. They said the fire department wouldn't let them go in and get them. "We're sorry, Mom. We couldn't get them," they said.

I said, "It's okay. We can get more birds. I'm just glad you guys are safe."

They got the fire out and things calmed down. I was thinking, by the looks of those flames, that it was done, that all our stuff was burnt up. When we got up close enough to actually see what had been on fire, it was the vacant apartment below us that had pretty much burnt it out. What? Well, to our surprise and by the mercy of Jesus, our apartment didn't burn, our things didn't burn, and guess what else? Through all the flames I saw, and all the smoke there was, both of the birds survived. All our things in the house where covered with soot, but everything was still there, and still okay. I had been sure it was our apartment on fire, and I had been sure our stuff would be gone—birds gone too—but no! God is so good. Wow!

The fire department told us a little later that we were really lucky that the kids had gotten out when they did because they would not have been able to make it past the flames. We just looked at each other and started crying again. We had a week of cleanup, but we were so grateful to the Lord that we were all safe, including the dog, and the birds, and we still had our little happy apartment. I'm telling you that was a God-send for it to work out just the way it worked out. No one other than Jesus could pull that off. Amazing God You are! Thank You!

"Enter through the narrow gate. For wide is the gate and broad is the road that leads to destruction, and many enter through it. But small is the gate and narrow the road that leads to life, and only a few find it" (Matthew 7:13–14).

Here is a very interesting story found on Godtube.com of a man we all know and love, Colonel Sanders and his faith in God.

It's no secret we have Colonel Sanders to thank for finger-lickin'-good chicken. But few know the actual facts behind the Kentucky Fried Chicken founder's hard fight to rise to culinary fame. It took a lifetime of self-discovery before Harland Sanders perfected the fried chicken recipe making him the legend he is today. But it wasn't until KFC founder Colonel Sanders accepted Jesus Christ into his heart that he finally felt true fulfillment. The Colonel's testimony just proves it's never too late to let God in.

Before he was given his honorary colonel title, presumably from the Kentucky governor, Harland Sanders was born into a poor family in 1890. His father died while the Colonel was a young age, and the boy helped his mother by feeding his siblings. The Colonel said "I did the cooking, and Mom did sewing for the neighbors," he recalled. "When I was seven, I baked my first bread. I cared for the two youngest while Mother worked." The Colonel's time spent in the kitchen would serve him well later in life. It would just take a while before he'd realize that cooking was one of his God-given talents.

The Colonel dropped out of school in the sixth grade. At sixteen he fibbed about his age and joined the army. He only served for six months before he was honorably discharged, which most likely was due to his age being discovered.

At eighteen, the Colonel married Josephine King of Jasper, Alabama. By the time he was nineteen, they were blessed with their first child, a baby girl named Margaret. Together they had three more children, but it wasn't long before the Colonel's lack of direction would take a toll on the marriage.

For most of Colonel Sanders's life, he was looking for a job, trying to find one that suited him. He tried being a farmer, streetcar conductor, soldier, railroad fireman, lawyer, an insurance salesman, steamboat operator, secretary, and a hotel and restaurant owner. He couldn't find his niche; he just didn't know what he was to be in life. At one point, Josephine took the kids and moved back with her parents; she was tired of his job jumping.

At this point, the Colonel was desperate and had thoughts of hiding in the woods near the parents' house and kidnapping the kids when they came out to play. But God was hard at work. The kids never came out, but Josephine's father did. He and the Colonel ended up having a deep conversation, and he was able to reconcile with his wife for a short time.

Finally, job after job again, he got a job in a cafe and ended up running it. After running it for several years, he ended up owning it. At sixty-five the Colonel sold his first restaurant and dedicated his time to developing the Kentucky Fried Chicken franchise. He had finally found his true calling. By seventy-three, the Colonel had sold the KFC corporation for two million dollars and was at last financially secure. But there still seemed to be something missing in his life, and he felt his searching was not quite finished yet. He was successful and he was satisfied with that, but he still yearned for more.

The Colonel started attending church and befriended a pastor by the name of Waymon Rogers. At one service, the pastor knelt down next to the Colonel, asking him if he'd like to be born again. "I really would," the Colonel replied. "Do you think that Jesus could save me and take away my cussing?" The Colonel was known for his pretty foul mouth.

Something amazing was about to happen that night at church. "God is going to save you tonight, Colonel, and you will never cuss again," Pastor Waymon told him. It was at that moment Colonel Sanders accepted Jesus into his heart. He told Pastor Waymon that he'd finally found the fulfillment he'd been looking for his whole life.

A few days later he told Pastor Waymon how everything had changed. "Since I prayed the sinner's prayer, things have completely changed in my life. I have not cussed even one time since then. It has really made me a new man."

From that point on, the Colonel allowed God to change him in many ways. He was baptized at age seventy-seven in the river Jordan and even experienced a divine healing. The Colonel was headed for surgery due to a growth on his colon. But the day he went in for surgery, he received incredible news. The doctor said that when he opened him up, the polyps were—gone. The Colonel knew this was a miracle from God.

As God worked in the Colonel's life, he developed a deep passion for giving back. He had worked his whole life to make his fortune, but after the Colonel accepted Jesus, he said, "I always figured there was no use to being the richest man in the cemetery." So the Colonel, at ninety, spent the rest of his days giving it all away.

This story just goes to show you that no matter how old you are, it's never too late to turn your life over to God.

** A HELPFUL HINT **

For a cold or stuffy nose.

Take a brown onion, with skin left on, and boil in 1–2 cups water.

Add bouillon, chicken or beef, and bring to a boil.

Let cool, and then drink. It will help clear your stuffy nose.

It's beyond amazing how God shows us His beautiful blessings. I hope you enjoy.

As my friend Betty, and I strolled around some plantation grounds in South Carolina, we found a trail leading off into the woods. It curved beneath moss-draped oaks that formed Gothic arches over our heads. The smell of heavily perfumed honeysuckle filled the air. Now and then we spotted a dogwood tree, its white blooms catching the light, and shimmering through the dense thicket.

"I feel like we are walking in a cathedral," I whispered.

"Aren't we?" Betty said.

We paused to admire a tuft of bridal wreath growing along the trail's edge. That's when she came—a black butterfly with a latticework of orange and blue on her wings. She lit on the toe of Betty's shoe and to our surprise began to crawl up her slacks and on the blouse she was wearing, all the way to the top of Betty's head. Then astonishingly, she flew to the top of my head and poised there before beginning a slow descent to my shoulder, then to the crook of my elbow. Not wanting to break the spell by speaking, Betty and I exchanged bemused glances. What was going on?

The butterfly wound down to the laces of my tennis shoe. On impulse I bent over and held my finger out to her the way you might offer it to a parakeet. The butterfly hopped right on. I lifted my finger until she was level with my nose. I had never been eye to eye with a butterfly before. It was as if I saw her through a magnifying glass: the large black hemisphere of her eyes, two tufts on either side of her mouth clothed in fuzzy hair, and the slender proboscis with which she drank the nectar of the woods. I know this will sound strange, but her gaze seemed fixed on me, as if she were as enthralled by me as I was by her. "Hello," I said softly.

We continued on through the woods together, Betty and I and this butterfly, who rode along on my finger and, for reasons we could not begin to fathom, seemed to be adopting us as her companions. Finally, Betty and I sat down on the ground in a clearing with our unlikely friend. She fluttered to Betty's shoulder, then back to my lap, where she performed graceful pirouettes across my kneecaps. She flitted about our heads, lit in our hair, and once she hung from Betty's earlobe like an earring.

Just when I thought she could amaze me no more, the butterfly flew to the crook of my neck and nestled there like a baby chick burrowing for protection beneath its mother's wing. As the butterfly opened and closed her wings, they grazed my throat like the brush of a baby's eyelashes, soft and barely perceptible, yet the vibration seemed to pulse through me. It felt a little like waking up. I remember a sense

of ignition inside, of being engulfed by a feeling of deep connection not only with this creature at my neck, but with the
whole natural world.

Later, when I had time to really think about it, I realized I had
been locked in a certain human egotism that pervades our
culture. I did not seem to understand that the butterfly and I
came from the same stuff of life; we were linked beyond my
wildest imaginings. I was suffering from a subtle estrange-
ment from the earth. I had forgotten the depth of my kin-
ship with it.

Such awakenings seem to come through deep encounters
with the self, through the medium of heart and soul. I have
heard it said that when Beethoven played his *Moonlight
Sonata* at a house concert for the first time, someone came
up afterward and asked, "What does this music mean?"

"I will tell you what it means," Beethoven said. Then he sat
down and played it again. Beethoven was saying what all
poets know: "that you arrive at the meaning of the music
through an experience of the music, not from an analysis
of it". Likewise, I arrived at my own form of eco-spiritual
awareness, not by funneling facts and information about the
despoliation of the earth into my head (though I'm sure that
wouldn't hurt), but by listening to the sunlight sonata of a
butterfly. In such ways, the poetry of creation enters us and
we are changed.

(Deuteronomy 6:5) says, "And you shall love the Lord your
God with all your mind and heart and with your entire being

and with all your might." In the New Testament, Jesus repeats this command and even points it out as the most important commandment of all, as well as loving your neighbor as yourself (Matthew 22:37–39). So how do we express our love for the Lord? Do we sing worship songs? Do we go to church? Do we read our Bible? These are all good things to do, but the best thing to do is just tell Him with a sincere heart, "I love You, God." The best way to show Him is through a relationship with Him. We want to spend time with those that we love, so it stands to reason that loving God will display itself in wanting to spend time with Him.

Being obedient to God's will is one of the highest forms of showing love for Him. Jesus said, "If you love Me, you will obey Me" (John 14:15).

One amazing thing about God is that He loves new beginnings. With God you don't have to live in bondage to yesterday and in fear of today. You can live in the beauty and promise of tomorrow. Scripture says that God's compassion and mercies are new every morning (Lamentations 3:23). God doesn't just allow do-overs—He created them! We can see that in the Word of God.

The more relationship you have with the Lord, the better you can see His path for you. Here's a few suggestions that might help to clear your mind and de-stress yourself:

1. Think of something pleasant.
2. Smile more.
3. Slow down.
4. Drink more water.
5. Eat a snack.

6. Finish a project before starting another.
7. Do something you enjoy.
8. Reevaluate your daily schedule.
9. Get a gift for someone else.
10. Tell yourself, "God loves me."

The Lord desires for our spirits to be light and free so we can function properly, not heavy or oppressed. He wants us to be encouraged to have confidence and to know we are unique in our own way. When you see someone with an amazing talent/gift, be thankful for their talent/gift, not jealous. You have your own unique talent/gift, and God's waiting for you to use it.

That's why it helps to clear your head and open your heart to your amazing and unique talents/gifts that you've been so graciously given. Think about what your heart's desires are, and expect to receive some sort of answer of where to go with whatever they are. He is amazing, so get ready to be amazed by Him. Praise and glory be to God for His unending love and faithfulness.

"I will praise you, for I am fearfully and wonderfully made; marvelous are your works, and that my soul knows very well" (Psalm 139:14).

What I Always Knew, but Now I Know #11

It was 2000, and I was still in Fairbanks. I met a lady named Laura at one of my brother's clubs, and we started talking. I found Laura to be a very interesting and smart lady. We discussed a little bit about ourselves and found out we had a lot in common. Basically, we just clicked. I could use a new friend, and Laura seemed to be a good one.

Days passed, and we talked more and more and got to know more and more about each other. I found out she was a masseuse—but not just a masseuse; she could do electro-massage. Electro-massage is where you don't need the masseuse to touch you to feel her energy penetrate your arm or leg. It was pretty neat, different, something I had never seen before, let alone know someone who could do it. It was cool. What a special gift!

Laura and I also had a love for the Lord in common. We talked a lot about the Lord, and His grace, and mercy. Time went on, and for some reason I started getting more of these feelings that I sometimes get. If I can describe it, it is like a puff of air hits your face and an overwhelming feeling comes over you, like you just know whatever it is that is going on— you just know. It's hard to explain, but I tried to explain it to Laura and she said, "I believe it. God is good and He gives us talents of many kinds." *I thought, Okay, but whatever kind of talent this is, I don't know the name!*

Anyway, Laura and I became really good friends and hung out quite often. On one particular day, Laura and I were going to go up in the mountains to see her friend who lived way up high on this mountain. It was snowing that day, and the temperature was in the twenties. Right before Laura was to pick me up to go, one of my overwhelming feelings came over me, and it was telling me not to go to the mountains, not today.

I called Laura quickly and told her about my feelings, and she said, "Okay, okay, we won't go if that's what you feel. Not a problem, I know it's for the best. I'm just going to stay in town and pay some bills, and we can go another day."

About an hour or so passed, and I got a phone call. It was Laura. She said, "Is there any way you can come pick me up and take me to my house? My car stalled and it won't start, and I had to have it towed to a garage."

With eyes big and my mouth open, I said, "I knew it. I knew something was wrong today. I knew it wasn't a good day to go anywhere."

She said, "Yep, you called it." But no, I didn't call it. See, that was a God-send. It probably happens to each one of us, but we just don't realize what it is and we don't connect with it. God is so amazing. Never underestimate the wonders of the Lord. We don't have to get it, but He knows what's up. Trust it!

What I Always Knew, but Now I Know #12

Same friend Laura but another day. Here we were again, going to that friend of Laura's who lived on the top of a mountain. This time we did make it up there and had a wonderful visit. I met another amazing lady and had a great time. It was getting late and was now time to leave, so off we went back down the mountain, heading home.

Just about five minutes into our drive down the mountain—*woosh*—that overwhelming feeling hit me, telling me to slow down and pull over. I told Laura as calmly as I could to please slow down and pull over—like now. She said "okay, okay". We slowed down and got ready to pull over, and right up ahead there was a momma moose on one side of the road and her baby on the other side. What I learned very quickly in Alaska was that if you see a momma moose and her baby, stay clear because the momma will get protective and will charge whatever is moving toward her baby.

Well, needless to say, we were basically on the top of the mountain, way up high on a dirt road covered with snow, and a cliff on one side. Laura said, "Oh my gosh! We could have been smashed if I would have kept going the speed I was going." We both held hands and got teary- eyed as we thanked our precious Jesus. After Momma crossed to her baby, off they went down the mountain. I'm telling you, God is an amazing Father who loves us so much. Listen to that voice! It's a God-send.

> *Dear God, thank You for sending these signs my way. I know that You love me and that You have a plan and purpose for my life. I also know that You have a purpose for the trials I've gone through and the trials I will face in the future. Give me the grace I need to go through the challenge, but also the grace to realize the lessons that You want me to learn. In Jesus' name, amen.*

Rest for Your Souls

"Come to me all who labor and are sorely burdened, and I will give you rest. Take My yoke upon You and learn from me because I am gentle and humble in heart, and you will find rest for your souls. For My yoke is easy and My burden is light". (Matthew 11:28–30)

I Am a New Creation in Him

"Therefore, if anyone is in Christ, he is a new creation. The old has gone, the new has come". (2 Corinthians 5:17).

What I Always Knew, but Now I Know #13

About six years ago, I became a foster mom to two boys; one ended up staying and the other didn't. Before I received any funding for this boy now gone, I had already spent well over three hundred dollars on clothes and a bicycle and other items he needed. Then he decided my rules and mother skills were not for him, so he went back to a group home.

When it was time for reimbursement from the foster care system for the funds spent, it seemed to be nothing but problems. It had been a hassle with this young man, as was the reimbursement. Finally, after two months had passed, they finally called and said they had a reimbursement check for me, but I would have to pick it up in person. Oh, geez—they were located in Los Angeles. Oh, man—I, the girl who gets turned around in Walmart, now had to drive to L.A. to get my money.

I tried to find someone, or at this point anyone, to make this trip with me, but I couldn't find anyone who was able to go with me. So I got the directions and off I went. I got down to the L.A area and I was so lost. I was hoping I had gotten off at the right exit in the right town, but really, I had no clue where I was or how far I still needed to go, or nothing. I was starting to get frustrated, and anxiety was setting in. I was almost in tears.

I was lost, so I pulled over and called my mom, telling her I was lost and I was frustrated. She could hear in my voice that I was obviously upset and about ready to cry. She said for me to just calm down and get it together. I asked her if she could get a map out and help me find where I needed to go. So she got a map out and said, "Okay, where are you? What town? What street? Can you see any addresses?" I said I had no clue, but thought I was in the right town.

Finally, I could see a sign but couldn't make out the name. My mom said, "What address are you looking for?" I read her the address (let's just say it was 4242), and she said, "Okay, what address are you at?"

I said, "4242," with as puzzled look as I could have. *Wait ... what?*

She said, "You are right there where you need to be."

I said, "No, Mom, I'm lost."

She said, "Well, you just told me the same address number."

It did take a couple of seconds for me to process it, and then ... OMG! I couldn't believe my eyes. I had pulled over right in front of the place I was trying to get to. My passenger door was directly in line with their front door. I started crying. I was in utter shock. What the ... ! I absolutely could not believe my eyes. I went into the office with my eyes all red from crying, and I tried to explain to the people in there. "You are not going to believe what just happened to me."

I proceeded to tell them, and they just looked at me strangely and said, "Oh cool. That worked out for you." I was standing there and I was thinking, *What! Cool?* No! They didn't understand what had just happened. It was not just cool; it was bizarre and truly *amazing*. It was God, for sure! How in the world could that have ever happened? I had no clue where I was, but God sure did. Only God! I was just in awe and cried again when I got back into my car to go home. Wow! When you have *no* explanation for something good that happens, it's simple—it's God.

Wings Of An Angel
Bird spread their wings as they leave their nest.
I'm spreading my prayers that you'll always be blessed.
Go fight and win the battle you didn't start,
on the wings of an angel's prayers from my heart.

Good and gracious God, we have no idea how marvelous You are. Open our eyes, our ears, and our hearts so we can begin to understand this. Amen

Thank You, Jesus, for my daughter Lacey. Please, Lord, let it be in Your will to allow her to see Your wonders and to hear the beauty of Your works. Strengthen both her and us to handle everything put before us. We pray You will be glorified through all of this. In Jesus' name we pray, amen.

God's Only Son

"God loved the world so much that He gave His only Son so that all who believe in Him might not be

99

destroyed but have eternal life. God did not send His Son into the world to judge the world, but through Him the world might be saved. One who believes in Him is not judged, but one who does not believe is judged already for not believing in the name of God's only Son". (John 3:16–18)

If you know the Lord and have been saved, your actions should show God. You won't always be able to do the right thing, because we all fall short and fall on our faces sometimes. Really, we are just saved sinners, but when you have Jesus in your heart, He knows when you're trying, and He will forgive you if you ask (1 John 1:9). When you fall, God will forgive you if you confess your sin. If you do fall, get back up and get back on the right track. Keep on keeping on.

God wants us to build on our salvation by pursuing holiness. It's not a negotiation with God. It's not a "don't call Me; I'll call you" deal. God wants us to call Him, and He says, "You call me and I'll listen."

"God is so eager for our holiness that He disciplines us for our own good" (Hebrews 12:10).

Here's a little comeback when you're telling people about Jesus and they respond in a negative way, like saying, "I shouldn't have had to go through that; God isn't fair."

What you tell them is, "You're right. You shouldn't have had to go through that. God isn't fair and I'm glad, because if He were fair, we wouldn't be here right now. We would be in hell."

What we need is God's love and mercy. If you want God's help, just ask Him. Tell the Lord you need Him (Proverbs 11:2). "Wisdom is given to the humble". Pray to God and say:

Lord, I need You in all I do. My paths are not clear when I try on my own. Lord, help me to see clearly through Your eyes. In Jesus' name, amen

Lord, please help me get on the right path, Your path, because Yours is the right and perfect path. Show me how to be humble and trust in You. You know what's up and You know what's best for me. In Jesus' name, amen

I pray, dear Lord, that You will fill me with the wisdom of Your holiness. Help me to be wiser than my enemies. Help me to fulfill Your will, not mine, for Your will is perfect. Lord, help me to trust You with all my heart and being. Help me to see things like You do. Help my heart to ask You for the things I desire, because if I don't ask You, You won't think that I want it very badly to begin with. In Jesus' name, amen

Lord, I also thank You for Your scars because without them I would be nothing. Thank You. And Lord, thank You for all my scars because I know who I was before, and without them I wouldn't know Your heart. Thank You. In Jesus' name, amen.

What I Always Knew, but Now I Know #14

A nother time in Fairbanks, Alaska, I was at work in the evening and had headed home for the evening. I got home, and right before I went to open my front door, I had that overwhelming feeling come over me again. For the next few minutes, I spoke words that I had no idea where they were coming from.

I opened the front door, and my daughter was on the phone. I had no clue whom she was talking to, but all of a sudden, I started telling her that the person she was talking to was being cheated on with a short, stocky, dark-haired girl. I could actually see her in my head. I was saying to her that the boyfriend was lying to her about where he was. It was so clear, what I was feeling and seeing, but it was a bit startling that I was not in control of what I was speaking. It was words coming out of me, but I know they were not my words. I had no clue; in fact, I had never even met this friend of my daughter's and didn't even know her name. I was so in awe of this incident.

I can't explain for sure what happened, but I do know that God is amazing and does things we may not understand at the time. But there is always a good reason for what He does. Was I supposed to save a heartache from growing bigger? I'm not sure what God's intention was on that, but I do know it was a divine intervention of some kind.

Lord, thank You for Your love and mercy, even when we don't understand it. I trust it because I trust You. In Jesus' name, amen

"O Lord, yea, though I walk through the valley of death, I will fear no evil. For Thou art with me; Thy rod and thy staff they comfort me" (Psalm 23:4).

"Praise ye the Lord. We give thanks unto the Lord, for He is good and His mercy endureth forever" (Psalms 106:1).

"The Lord is my light and my salvation; whom shall I fear? The Lord is the strength of my life. Of whom shall I be afraid? Wait on the Lord, be of good courage, and He shall strengthen thine heart. Wait, I say, on the Lord" (Psalm 17:11–14).

Today I Saw Him

Today on the highway I saw Him, He gazed up and smiled at me.
Today on the highway I found Him, Jesus of Galilee.
So gentle and kind was His manner,
And though He made never a sound, I felt as I gazed upon Him,
That I stood in the presence of divine, the very same Jesus who suffered,
The very same Jesus who died.
Today on the highway I found Him, He gazed up and smiled at me.

Dear God, thank You for giving us so many examples in the Bible. Thank You that the men and women in the Bible were just like me. I am grateful to understand that I can overcome the trials in life just like they did as I keep my eyes on You. Help me to see trials as a way to grow and develop into Your image. In Jesus' name, amen.

The Jordan River crossings teach us that God's ways are better than our own. The method God used to get Joshua and the people across the flooded river, miraculously holding back the river's flow and allowing the people to cross on dry ground, was something even the most experienced or creative leader couldn't have fathomed. It wasn't remotely possible in the human realm. But with God *all* things are possible. God's ways are higher than ours. Always remember that.

Sometimes we face rivers just ahead of us, with no real plan for the crossing. We strategize, we stress out, and we worry, but we still come up with no really good plan. Just how do we cross our Jordan? In modern terms, the Jordan River we face represents a challenge, a dilemma, a tragedy, or a heartbreak that comes our way when we least expect it. These are the things of life that catch us off guard and cause distress, much like the day in November when my sister was killed and in May when my dad went home to be with the Lord.

God doesn't mess around; He's got it all under control. Think of what He did in that place. Moments before, the waters raged, but now the ground was dry—not muddy, not slippery, but dry! That's the deliverance God offers. Make no mistake; we all have raging rivers or trials to face. Sometimes the examination is so great and our strength is so small that we feel overwhelmed. The trials and challenges we face have purpose: to give Him the opportunity to miraculously deliver us and make us stronger. They are tests, but God has given us everything we need to meet the challenge. With God's help, we can cross any river, overcome any obstacle. We can rise to the occasion if we allow God's promises to flow through us.

Dear God, I recognize that You are what I need when I face the smooth-flowing streams of life, and You are what I need when I face the raging rivers of testing. Thank You that You have promised to never leave or forsake me. Thank You that You have promised even to be close to me when I go through trials and testing. In Jesus' name, amen.

Talking about Jesus is so easy to do that I could go on for days of all the beautiful things He does for us. His love is so loving, His grace is so graceful, His mercy is so merciful, His miracles are so miraculous. His dying on the cross is the undying truth, and His forever is eternity.

What are your goals in life? What do you feel God has called you to accomplish? What do you know God has gifted you to do? Have you gotten as far or done as much as you'd hoped? It's okay if you haven't arrived yet; God's still working in your life. It's His strength, not yours, that matters. Don't get discouraged. Stay strong and keep striving for spiritual growth. God's still working on you.

Remember, as I said earlier, when people are too tired to give you a smile, give them one of yours. Sometimes a smile means so much, and it doesn't cost a thing to give it. Sometimes your smile can make someone feel loved, or sometimes your smile gives hope, or sometimes your smile may save a life. Try to smile a little more so someone can stress a little less.

What I Always Knew, but Now I Know #15

O ne day I went to Walmart to get a few things for my mom. It was going to be a trip for just a few items. There weren't very many people in the store that day, so I figured this was really going to be quick. I got started shopping and found all the things she needed, and I was heading toward the checkout when all of a sudden, I noticed my purse was gone. I had to think for a minute, *Did I leave it in the car?* Then it hit me—someone had just stolen my purse from right under my nose. Everything was in it: my keys, my address, my credit cards, my cell phone, and my money. I had kept my purse right in front of me, so how could this happen? But it did.

I headed toward the security guard, shaking, panicking, and holding back tears. I felt so invaded and a little in disbelief. But it was definitely reality. It was gone. Then it hit me again that whoever did this had my car keys, and all they would have to do to find the car was to hit the lock button on the key, so I headed outside. Then I was scared they might rob my house because they had my house keys with my address on my driver's license. I was panicking badly.

I was standing at the back of my car; security had called the police, and we were waiting for them to arrive. Then I asked to use the security's phone to call my daughter to come to Walmart and pick me up after the police took the report. About ten minutes went by, and I was leaning on the back of my car, praying, *Please, Jesus, let this be okay. Please let this be okay.* I was half crying and half still in shock.

I kept praying, and all of a sudden, a lady came up and put her hand on me and started praying for me. She then told me, "Honey, whatever was in your purse is replaceable, but the love Jesus has for you is much bigger. He will take care of you."

I said, "Thank you, ma'am. I know He loves me," and I pointed to my license plate that read, "He died for me, I will live for Him." I said, "Thank you, ma'am. I appreciate that." She then handed me forty dollars, but I told her, "No, ma'am, thank you, but I don't want your money."

She said, "Please take this. I want to give it to you. Please take it." I thanked her, and off she went. I don't know where she came from or how she knew what was going on, but she did. I did feel better after she left; I felt a calm came over me.

I was standing at my car waiting for the police to arrive, and all of a sudden, my daughter came driving up with a strange look on her face. She was on her cell phone talking to someone. I saw her walking quickly toward me, and she said, "Mom, your purse is at Grandma's house!"

I said, "What? What do mean at Grandma's house?"

She said, "A lady returned your purse to Grandma's house. She said she found it at a bus stop and thought it looked strange to see a purse sitting there, so she picked it up and looked inside for an address or a phone number. She found a license and brought it to that address."

I was in an even bigger shock now. The address she was looking at was on an old license that I still had in my wallet for some reason, and it had my mom's address on it, not mine. The funny thing about that is if she would have found my current license, it would have had my current address on it, and I wouldn't have been there for her to return the purse to me.

The police arrived, and we proceeded to let them know the purse had been returned to my mom's house. I think they were in as much shock as I was that it was returned so quickly. Oh my gosh, my daughter drove us over to my mom's, which seemed to be one of the longest rides ever, even though it was only a couple of miles away.

We got there, and I was half in shock, half crying, and half amazed that God had heard me and answered so quickly. Wow! There was my purse with keys in it, cell phone in it, and my wallet in it with all my credit cards and important stuff. All I could do was cry with thankfulness to God. Everything was in my purse but the money I had in there, which was about sixty dollars. I had been saving for food for the homeless, so the money they took was not my bill or rent money. It was extra anyway; it just went to the wrong people.

I was sitting there at my mom's, getting ready to go back up to Walmart to get my car, when the mail arrived, and guess what? There was a child support check in the mail. (That's a strange story in itself.) With the amount of the check and the forty dollars the lady gave me, I had a hundred dollars more than I had before I made the trip to Walmart. Wow, God—You are so good and amazing!

So there you go. It just goes to show you that when the Lord said that He will take care of us and give us tenfold in blessings, He wasn't kidding. It was absolutely amazing that I got my purse back with everything in it before the police ever took a report. Thank You, Jesus, for such a quick answer to my prayer. You sure made it all right, Lord, just as I had prayed.

> "If any of you lack wisdom, he should ask God, who gives generously to all without finding fault, and it will be given to him" (James 1:5).

> "This you know, my beloved brethren. Let every man be quick to hear, slow to speak, and slow to anger, for the anger of man does not achieve the righteousness of God" (James 1:19–20).

I pray that you will stay focused on our great and wonderful Savior. I pray that your love will grow, your faith will grow, and you will never stop wanting to know more and more about our creator of the universe. He never stops thinking and being with each of us, and He is the one who died for us. You know what conclusion I have come up with? I have come to the understanding that since *God died for me, I will live for Him.*

Lord, I am just in awe of You, now and forevermore. I will repeat this and repeat this until the day I die, and then if I am able to speak when I meet You, Lord, I will tell You, "Jesus I love You, and I am in awe of You now and forevermore".

Poem Written by Devyn Williams

Your love feeds my soul,
Only Your love makes me whole.

No matter how far I go,
You are always in control.
Jesus, I love You.
I feel peace in my heart,
I wish I would have accepted it from the start.
But now I know,
That I'm never alone.
So I'm getting down on my knees,
To show I'm pleased with my King.
I bow down to You for everything You have done for me,
Jesus, I love You.
Only You can make me feel this way,
Making me feel whole again,
When you wash my sins away.
Jesus, I love You.

Each real-life story that we share is designed to turn your secrets into spoken dreams and your spoken dreams into reality. May the constant reminder of being created according to God's design and for His distinct pleasure stay fresh in your heart and mind every minute of every day. May your journey find you opening your eyes, opening your heart, and opening the door to a whole new way of loving God and serving others. "Before a word is on our tongue, You know it completely. "For I know the plans I have for you," declares the Lord, "plans to prosper you and not to harm you, plans to give you hope and a future" (Jeremiah 29:11).

Dear Lord, I pray for young children starving in a nation so overfed. It's more obscene than pornography.

Did you know we are given value just for being God's son or daughter?

Giving to God what is God's is ultimately about placing the most valuable things we have in trust with Him:

1. Our identity/sense of self
2. Our direction and how we move toward our goals
3. Our destiny and final outcome of life

Where does your identity lie: in the job you do? in the family you make? in the book you write? in the relationships you have? Your identity should lie in the one and only God of the universe.

Lord, I don't want regrets. I want to know I did what pleased You. The glorious destiny is the Lord calling us to the final chapter. Remember, God is the author; He knows the whole story!

What I Always Knew, but Now I Know #16

M y second daughter, Lacey, is thirty-three, and right before Christmas 2018, she was diagnosed with leukemia. The doctors said that her type of leukemia, acute myeloid leukemia, is very rare for someone her age. It usually attacks someone who is sixty-five or older. But she has it and has been going through chemotherapy for the past six months. Even through all of the chemotherapy, blood transfusions, and platelet transfusions, God has been so merciful and loving.

The first couple of rounds of chemo were pretty bad. Lacey got really sick, lost her hair, and was very neutropenic for weeks. *Neutropenic* means that her blood counts, both red and white, were so low she was in danger of catching anything and everything and even had to eat certain foods because of the bacteria some foods contain. The red cells are what gives your body the oxygen it needs, and the white blood cells fight off infections. So needless to say, we have been praying overtime, and I know God hears us. He is such an amazing, loving Father.

He has been there with us every step of the way so far, and I know He will be there with us even more in the days to come. He continues to answer our prayers to keep Lacey from becoming sick this round of chemo and continues to show us His presence through all of this. To tell you how I know for a fact that Jesus is right there and hears us is because our prayers continue to be answered and answered again; for example, when they told Lacey she was a candidate for a bone marrow transplant—thank You, Jesus.

Some leukemia patients aren't able to have a bone marrow transplant due to being too weak, too far advanced, not in remission, or a right donor can't be found to do the transplant. But praise Jesus again and again! Lacey is not too weak, the leukemia hasn't advanced, and she is in remission. Praise Jesus; thank You, Father God! The transplant needs to be done as soon as possible because the chances of the leukemia coming back between her rounds of chemotherapy are very high, and with a high chance of it attacking the brain if it returns.

As we were praising the Lord and thanking our heavenly Father for His love and mercy, we were also continuing to pray for the next step of finding a donor. They first start with full-blooded siblings; then they go to parents, then half siblings, then other family members, and then to the donor list. So, okay, Lacey has a full-blooded sibling, a younger brother, Devyn, and of course Devyn was more than willing to help his sister in any way he could.

The hospital sent him a bone marrow kit to do a swab test. He did the test, which consisted of him swabbing his mouth and putting the sample in a sealed container and sending it back. He sent it in, and then they waited for Lacey's swab test. The odds of a match between blood siblings are approximately 25 percent, or you could also say a 1 out of 4 chance of there being a match of any kind. What they are in hopes of is that if there is a match of any kind, that it will be at least 60 percent or better to be able to proceed with the transplant, because if it's less than that, the chances of it taking are slim. The higher the match, the better it is for the transplant to succeed.

What happened next was a *miracle from our heavenly Father.* We got the swab tests back, and wow! Not only was her brother, Devyn, a match, but he was an absolute 100 percent match for Lacey. Yes, you read it right—100 percent match.

Oh my Lord Jesus, You are so awesome, loving, kind, and merciful. I am so grateful to You, and I honor Your name and Your great works. They are truly, truly a blessing and a miracle from You. I love You, Father God.

Thank You, Lord, for loving my baby and putting Your mighty arms all around her. You are so mighty and powerful, and I am so weak and powerless. Lord, I needed You then, I need You now, and I need You always. Every minute of every day, I need You and I love You. I know without a doubt in my being that it is *You and only You who is mighty enough and powerful enough to pull this off.* Thank You, Lord, thank You.

———————————————◆———————————————

I did a little research from the National Cancer Institute on leukemia and bone marrow transplants, and I jotted down the statistics for donors just to give you a little insight on this horrific disease. But even more than that, I would like to give you insight on *the miracle from God—the match.*

This year more than 130,000 people will be diagnosed with a serious blood disease. Leukemia (blood cancer) will strike 44,000 people this year, including 3,500 children. It will kill about half of the adults and about 700 of the children.

Leukemia is the most common childhood cancer, but there are many types of leukemia. Some affect the elderly more, and some affect the young, but it basically has no age limit. Only 30 percent of people needing a bone marrow transplant have a matching donor in their family. The odds of a donor match with all donors are 1 in 430 and are based on the leukocyte antigen, which is each individual tissue type. This is the most important factor for the match. The odds again are 30 percent. The remaining 70 percent must hope that a compatible stranger can be found in the donor registry.

At any given time, about 7,500 people are searching the national registry hoping that they can come up with any kind of match, even if it's minute. But the odds of a minute match prevailing are slimmer; this would be in the range of a 40–50 percent match. Doctors rarely continue with this percentage. Did you know that only 2 percent of the people in the world are on the national registry donor list? Statistics show that only 1 percent of all donors are bone marrow donors, and most of them cannot be located or will not follow through with the process when asked to do so. If willing and available, the percentages are 65 percent Caucasian, 47 percent Hispanic, 44 percent Asian, 34 percent African American, and 10–20 percent multiracial. Three thousand people die each year because they can't find a donor.

Seventy percent of blood marrow donations use the peripheral blood stem-cell apheresis, which means drawing it out like giving blood. Thirty percent of donations use the traditional method of putting a needle in your hip.

Donating bone marrow is safe. More than 35,000 people have donated bone marrow to a stranger without a single donor death. Common sense suggests that if there were moderate incentives, there might be more people willing to donate bone marrow. But the federal law makes it a felony punishable by up to five years in prison.

That's why on October 28, 2009, adults with deadly blood diseases, the parents of sick children, a California nonprofit, and a world-renowned medical doctor who specializes in bone marrow search joined with the Institute for Justice to launch a legal fight against the U.S. attorney general to put an end to a ban on offering compensation for bone marrow donors. In other words, people would be paid, just like when they donate blood. It replenishes itself.

The National Organ Transplant Act (NOTA) of 1984 treats compensation for marrow donors as though it were black-market organ sales. Under the NOTA, payment for donating bone marrow would land everyone in jail—the doctor, nurse, patient, and donor—for up to five years in prison. Of course, that would be very harsh to receive.

The NOTA criminal ban violates equal protection because it basically treats renewable bone marrow like nonrenewable solid organs instead of like other renewable or inexhaustible cells, such as blood, for which compensation is legal. This makes no sense. Bone marrow, unlike organs such as kidneys, replenishes itself in just a few weeks after it is donated, leaving the donor whole again. The ban also violates the right to participate in safe, accepted, life-saving and otherwise legal medical treatment.

On December 1, 2001, the Ninth Circuit Court ruled in favor of holding the National Organ Transplant Act ban on donor compensation. They ruled no pay for donors. Then the U.S. attorney general tried to have the ruling overturned but was unsuccessful. But our victory became final in June 2012, When they decided it would be legal to donate bone marrow

with no cost to the patient or the donor. That is why today we are allowed to still give bone marrow on our own free will, but there will be no compensation for it. You get paid for sperm, eggs, donating blood or carrying someone else's baby, but you don't get paid to help save a life. But let me just say this: the payment is in saving a human life. Take that to the bank!

Needless to say, you see the circumstances regarding this horrific disease. The percentage of donors and matches is incredibly low and difficult to find. So when you see a 100 percent match with anyone at any time, it is most definitely a miracle from our precious God. Not only was Devyn a match for Lacey, but he was an *identical match in tissue*, a possibility more rare than not. There is only one explanation for this perfected percentage—our *perfect God*, our Lord Jesus Christ, and no other. I am so beyond grateful.

———————————————————◆———————————————————

What we think and feel about God is absolutely essential in praying effectively. We need to be thoroughly in agreement that God is good. There is more to this than just casually praying. Being deeply rooted in the truth, believing for the miraculous, and persevering for God's goodness must be in our hearts and minds. He knows what's in our hearts; He created us.

"Most assuredly, I say to you, he who believes in Me, the works that I do he will do also; and greater works than these will he do, because I go to My Father" (John 14:12).

I've heard of people getting mad at God and saying they don't believe in Him anymore because of something bad happening to them and they blame God for it. I don't mean to sound coldhearted or anything, but you can't turn God on and off, not in that way. You might accuse Him of your heartache and refuse to serve Him, and you have that free choice because of Him. But you can't decide He no longer exists. Even if you claim you want nothing to do with Him, or that He isn't real, it doesn't get rid of Him. It's impossible for us to understand, perceive, describe, or imagine the power of God. It would take us all of eternity to try.

"And do not be conformed to this world, but be transformed by the renewing of your mind, so that you may prove what the will of God is, that which is good and acceptable and perfect" (Romans 12:2).

The Lord is compassionate and gracious, slow to anger and abounding in loving kindness. He will not always strive with us, nor will He keep His anger forever. He has not dealt with us according to our sins, nor rewarded us according to our iniquities. For as high as the heavens are above the earth, so is His loving kindness toward those who fear Him. "As far as the east is from the west, so far has He removed our transgressions from us. Just as a Father has compassion for His children, so the Lord has compassion on those who fear Him" (Psalm 103:8–13).

"The Lord isn't slow in keeping His promise, as some understand slowness. Instead, He is patient, with God not wanting anyone to perish, but everyone to come to repentance" (2 Peter 3:9).

"These things I have spoken to you so that in Me you have peace. In the world you have tribulation, but take courage; I have overcome the world" (John 16:33).

"Do not let your heart be shaken. Believe in God and believe in Me. In My Father's house there are many rooms. If there were not, why would I have said to you then that I go to prepare a place for you? And if I go to prepare a place for you, I will come and take you to Me so that where I am you may also be. And where I go you may know the way. I am the way, the truth, and the life. No one comes to the Father but through Me. If you knew Me you would have also known My Father, and now you know Him and have seen Him" (John 14:1–7).

"This is my command, that you love each other as I have loved you. No one has greater love than this, than to lay down one's life for one's friends. You are My friends if you do what I command you. No longer will I call you slaves, because the slave does not know what the master does. But you I have called friends because all the things I have heard from My Father I have made known to you. You did not choose Me, but I chose you and appointed you to bear fruit, and your fruit will last. And so whatever you ask for in My name He may give you. These things I command you so you may love one another" (John 15:12–17).

What I Always Knew, but Now I Know #17

I used to work for a company called Jerry Leigh, as I mentioned in an earlier God-send. Jerry Leigh is a company that makes Disney clothing. It is a pretty neat company and makes awesome clothes. I used to stop every morning, or at least almost every morning, at a little donut shop close by my work and would get a coffee or hot chocolate, depending on what my taste was for that day, and a bagel or a donut, again depending on my taste for that day.

This went on for weeks, and then one day I noticed a homeless person all wrapped up and sleeping in the doorway of a business a couple of doors down from the donut shop. As I was buying my daily treats, I start feeling selfish for buying something and not buying the homeless person anything. So I got the same exact thing I had gotten that morning and set it next to the homeless person.

I never saw whether it was a man or a woman; the person was always wrapped up sleeping when I got there, as it was pretty early in the morning. For a couple of weeks, I still didn't know whether it was a man or a woman I was leaving this stuff for. Then one morning the person was awake, still all wrapped up, and I'm sad to say very filthy. I still couldn't tell whether it was a man or a woman, but I spoke and said good morning. The person didn't answer back, so I kept walking and went to buy my usual morning stuff, along with that extra for the homeless person. I got it and took it to them and set it down as I usually did, and this person said, "Thank you."

I said, "You are so welcome. God bless, and I will see you tomorrow," and off I went to work.

The next day I repeated what I did every morning, but now this morning, after I set the coffee down, the person, who I now knew was a man, said to me, "Thank you."

I said, "You're very welcome. What is your name?"

He said, "Cherry, like the fruit."

I said, "Well it's very nice to meet you, Cherry. My name is Teresa, and I just wanted to share breakfast with you even though you were always sleeping." I told him, "I figured when you wake up, you would be hungry." He never did mention to me about all the other times I had left the treats for him.

Now I was getting to know this man named Cherry, and I started to buy him food. Every paycheck I got I would go and buy him twenty-five dollars' worth of food and toiletries. Sometimes I bought him clothes and shoes and socks and other basic things most of us take for granted. This went on for a few months; twice a month I tried to help this man as much as I was able.

Now it was Christmas time, and I could not get Cherry off my mind, thinking of him sleeping in the entryway of that business and not having a family to share Christmas with. So I went and spent over two hundred dollars on nice clothes, more shoes, a new Bible, lots of food, cologne, and just a bunch of things you would need or want if you had a home. My son helped me wrap everything up. I mean, we wrapped everything and wrapped them each individually because I wanted him to have as many presents as I could give him to open. I thought it would be more exciting, and I sure hope he thought that.

Anyway, we went and gave the gifts to him, and he started crying, telling me he was so grateful and how much he appreciated it. By the way, he was a very, very nice man who had just gotten himself stuck in a bad situation and didn't know how to pull out of it. We left after dropping off the presents and went home.

Christmas came and went, and I went back to work after a few days of vacation and repeated my routine at the donut shop. I expected to see my friend Cherry, but to my surprise, Cherry was not there this particular morning. I was sad and wondered, *Where did he go?* I looked all over for him, but I couldn't find him. I was so sad all day—my friend was gone.

The next day I went again to get my treats, and there was a man standing by the donut shop, clean and nicely dressed in what I thought to be familiar clothes. It was Cherry. He was all cleaned up and dressed in new clothes we had given him for Christmas; he looked so sharp and was just glowing. I said, "Cherry, is that you?" Of course, I knew it was him. I was just trying to boost his ego.

He said, "Yes, it's me, Teresa."

I said, "You look amazing! Where did you go? I was so worried about you. I came by yesterday and you weren't here."

He said, "Nope, I don't live there anymore." I thought he was going to tell me they had kicked him away from the entryway, but no, that wasn't it, because his face was grinning from ear to ear. He said, "I got a job."

I said, "What? You did? That is wonderful!"

He said he got a job cleaning in front of the entryways of all the businesses along the street right there by the donut shop, and that he was now going to be able to rent a room instead of being on the street. He cried, thanking me again for all I had done for him, and wanted to give me a gift to thank me.

I told him, "Cherry, you don't have to do that."

He said, "Please let me give you something to say thank you." I was so humbled and honored that he would give me a gift. I knew it was from deep in his heart. It was a brand-new American flag, a huge flag.

I started crying, not because of what he had given me, but because here was this man who had nothing but who managed to get a new flag to thank me for my kindness. He said if it weren't for all I had done for him, he wouldn't have been able to pick himself up and move on.

I told him, "It wasn't me, Cherry. It was the good Lord who allowed me to be able to do those things for you. Please tell Him thank you."

Then he said the best words I could have ever heard. He said, "I know it was Him. I have been thanking Him. I've been getting to know Him from the Bible you bought me for Christmas, so does that make you my angel?"

I was speechless, but my heart was screaming with joy. I felt such a peace and contentment come over me; it felt like a blanket of love covering me. I know it was God because it felt so perfect, so right, so peaceful. It's hard to explain the feeling.

I was bawling, he was bawling, and we hugged each other. For the next week, I saw a changed man. It was beautiful. My heart was just smiling, and I was so grateful I was able by the grace of God to help this man. It was just a fuzzy feeling in my heart. I remember being so proud of Cherry.

Then, for a couple days, I didn't see Cherry again, so I asked the donut shop what had happened to him. They said, "Oh, Cherry? He got a good job across town." He was now working for a grocery store, collecting carts. I did go across town a couple of times looking for him, but I never found him, and that was the end of ever seeing Cherry again. But the story doesn't end there.

Remember the flag I told you he gave me? Well, my Aunt Virgie, who worked for a school, a couple of days after I was given the flag, told my mom that her school was in need of a flag for their flagpole in front of the school. My mom mentioned it to me and I said, "Mom, you're not going to believe this, but I have a new flag she can have."

She said, "Where in the world did you get a huge flag like that?" I told her how I had gotten it, and she was amazed.

What is even more amazing, though, was the fact that Cherry ended up rising up from the ground and flying high like that flag. Not only was Cherry now free of his homeless bondage, but he was now learning about Jesus and how to free his soul. Wow! What a lump in the throat. Fly free, my friend, until we meet again someday.

God, You are simply divine. Helping this man did more for me than he could ever know, and he thought I was helping him.

Angels may not always come when you call them, but they come when you need them.

Lord, I ask You with Your divine power and loving touch,
Please make me an instrument of Your peace.
Please show me how to love, not hate.
Please help me to have faith and not doubt.
Please show me hope and not despair.
Please help me to stay in the light and out of darkness.
Please show me how to be happy and not sad.
Please help me trust in You and nothing else.
Please show me Your way and not my own.
Please help me be strong and not weak.
Please show me I am loved when I feel rejected.
Please help me to be more like You and not like me.
Please show me through Your eyes, not through mine.
Please help me to know You Like You know me.
Please show me how to be humble, not proud.
Please help me to be quiet when I need not speak.
Please show me I have strength when I feel I can't go on.

Lord, I ask You with Your divine power and loving touch to help me, show me.

———————◆———————

I hope that while you have been reading this book that you have had many different emotions. Maybe you found something in here just to think about, or maybe you found something in here that made you laugh, or maybe you read something in this book that made you cry, or maybe you will remember a story in here that will help you long after you have read the book. I want whoever reads this book to know that it's more than just a book with a simple story. I want it to have layers with meaning and depth. I would like to know that something in this book hits home or hits possibly the center of your heart. Then I will know I have achieved my goal. The goal is to share the wonderful creator and His marvelous works. That is my whole goal of this book. I wrote this book, but Jesus is the author.

When I read my Bible, I try to memorize certain scriptures, but it confuses me a little and frustrates me when I can't keep them memorized. So I don't try to memorize them as much anymore; I just read them slowly and try to absorb the meaning and try my best to understand.

Sometimes I feel like Satan is trying to take my enjoyment out of reading the Word or making me feel like there is no use to pray. But then I think about the truth, and it fires me right back up to continue to read my Bible and continue to pray, because that is how we obtain the spirit of prayer. The more I pray, the more I desire it, and the more I read the Word, the more I desire to read it.

God is the source of the Bible, and the Bible is true. Once you realize it holds the answers to life's questions, you will probably have a bigger desire to read it. Don't try to rush the reading, though, because it will fade. Instead, try to take it easy. Take your time and focus on the divine words of our creator, the true words of our creator. Dig deep so you can absorb the truth deep within your core being; let it fill your every cell. That's why I am convinced that we were created for the Word—not just to hear it or read it, but to let it soak in, inhale it, live it, be it. "The Word of God is living and active" (Hebrews 4:12).

Knowing God, even a mustard seed of faith, is enough to grow on, just like an apple, orange, or lemon seed. So here it is: All you need is some good soil; then you dig a hole, put your seed in, cover it up, and water it. Every day you go out and you water that seed, and pretty soon you see something start to sprout. Every day you water it, and it grows a little more each day. Pretty soon then you have a small tree. Then you add more water, and now the tree grows leaves. You start to talk to it, which does help it grow. I'm pretty sure that helps, but even if it doesn't, it makes you feel better by doing it, right? Now your little tree is getting really big, and guess what? It has little fruits on it—good job! Your tree-growing is working; it's bearing fruit. The tree grows bigger now and is just loaded with fruit. The fruit is getting riper and sweeter by the day. Now it has so much fruit you have no other choice but to share it with others, and it's bearing so much fruit that others are making jam out of it, where it spreads even farther. So now the ones you shared the fruit with got a taste of that fruit and jam, and now they want to grow a tree of their own because they see how your tree is growing and how good its fruit tastes.

Let me explain this a little better. You have a mustard seed of faith, enough to grow on. Good soil = a good will, to dig a hole = open your heart, to cover it with dirt = God's love. Water it every day = read the Word and pray. Then the seed sprouts = the Lord is growing in your heart. So you water it some more = learning about the Lord even more. Now you start to see leaves = Holy Spirit filling your heart. Now you start talking to your plant = you start having an intimate relationship with the Lord. Now the tree is really growing = your faith is really growing. Now there is fruit on the tree = blessings you start noticing. Now the fruit is growing in abundance = talents and gifts are surfacing. Now the fruit is getting ripe and ready to pick = your knowledge to evangelize. Now there is so much fruit to share = sharing about the victory of salvation. Now your friends see all the fruit = you're acting out godly ways. Now they have to make jam with so much fruit = spreading the Word to more friends. Now they want a tree of their own = their mustard seed of faith. And the trees continue to spread and grow = more and more people coming to Jesus.

A mustard seed is all you need to grow a beautiful tree. Now the orchard has begun. It goes on and on and from one person to another, just like an infectious disease. Only it's just the opposite—it's an infectious dose of life. And that, my friend, is how I describe what I would like my mustard seed to be. It's a process and I am still growing, but I am bearing fruit that is getting sweeter every day. Do you have your seed? Are you ready to plant it? What's holding you back? The weather is perfect today. Get your seed planted, water it, and watch it grow. For further instructions on planting, please refer to (Matthew 17:20) and (Romans 20:9).

Fruit has two important qualities. The first quality is the type of fruit the tree bears. The second thing is when it bears fruit in abundance, it should always be shared with others because when people see your fruit, they will want to taste it. Then other people will want to grow their own trees that bear fruit so they can share the great flavor.

> "You did not choose Me, but I chose you and appointed you so that you might go and bear fruit, fruit that will last, and so whatever you ask in My name the Father will give you" (John 15:16).

> "And He is the image of the invisible God, the first Son of all creation. For by Him all things were created both in the heavens or on earth. Visible or invisible, all things have been created by Him for Him" (Colossians 1:15–16).

> "The heavens declare the glory of God and the sky displays what His hands have made" (Psalm 19:1).

How can anyone reject the love or the existence of God? After seeing the world of creation and all the things that make life what it is, it's sufficient enough for me. What about you? What I see is there is none like Him, the almighty God. When God wants to do something, He just does it (Ephesians 1:5). God does all things out of Himself simply because it pleases Him to do so.

Having a relationship with Jesus enhances our worship. Even though He doesn't need to be worshiped to love us, we worship Him because we love Him. God doesn't need us—we need Him, just like we need parents. Have you ever told your kids, "I am the parent; you are the child. You don't tell me; I tell you"? That's pretty much how I see it with the Lord. He is telling us He is the Father and we are His children. Since there is nothing greater than the Lord, you'd better saddle up. This is God's rodeo, and you, cowboy, are going for a ride.

As you well know, God can do things we can't even think of doing. When it comes to defending God, we defend Him when we hear people bashing His name. But God doesn't need defending; we just do it because we love Him and know His love, and it hurts our hearts just as if someone was bashing our parents here on earth. We don't like it; it hurts. Romans 12:19 says, "Vengeance is mine, sayeth the Lord. I will repay, says the Lord. I can do things you haven't even thought about." Yikes, I don't want to be at the end of that deal. Knowing the power of God and to be His enemy scares the bejeebers out of me. No, thank you. I will pass on that deal. I'm sticking to Jesus' team. He always wins!

Well, I have another God-send for you. Are you ready to hear more amazing things the Lord can do? Here it goes.

What I Always Knew, but Now I Know #18

I was sixteen years old and had just recently gotten my driver's license. On this particular day, I was on my way home from school. Just before I got home, I saw a neighbor lady, Mrs. Huebner, sitting at the corner of the school across from my house with one of her children and a couple of bags of groceries. She had a look on her face like she was worn-out and couldn't walk another step, poor thing. Mrs. Huebner was a lady who lived behind us a couple of blocks. She was a single mother raising seven or eight children, and I had gone to school with a couple of her kids. I had never met Mrs. Huebner in person, but I knew who she was from her children and because she used to walk everywhere, pushing her little wire basket, since she didn't drive. I asked her if she would like a ride home, and she said, "Yes, I would, honey. Thank you." So I gave her a ride home, and that was that. This was the only time this precious lady and I ever came face-to-face until …

Fast forward thirty-two years later. I was attending a funeral for a friend of mine in a little dinky church in town. I mean, it was little. It had only five or six pews on each side of the church, with hymn books in the back of each one. A little old lady was playing the organ with really old songs, like "The Old Rugged Cross." You can almost picture the scene, right? It was just a little old- fashioned church with old-fashioned ways; it was so adorable. It reminded me of the church in the TV show *Little House on the Prairie*. I love that show.

Anyway, the service went on with more old songs, which, by the way, were great songs. There was nothing wrong with that; they were golden oldies. Then it was time to share some food and share some stories of our friend. I saw the little old lady who was the organ player standing there, and I went over to her to tell her how lovely her organ playing was, and guess who it was? It was Mrs. Huebner. Oh my gosh! I hadn't seen her for years and years, thirty-two to be exact. I wasn't sure if she had moved or if she still lived a few blocks behind my mom's house.

I said to her, "Hello, Mrs. Huebner. I don't know if you know who I am, but I am an old neighbor of yours. I went to school with a couple of your kids. I used to live across from the school."

She said to me, "Honey, I remember you. You gave me a ride home one day when I couldn't walk another step."

I said, "I did? Oh!"

She said, "I have never forgotten that."

I couldn't remember ever doing that, but okay. I was sitting down eating some food and trying to rack my brain for when I had ever given her a ride home. I couldn't remember it. Then all of a sudden, it hit me, and I nearly choked on my food. I was thinking, *Oh my word! I remember it now. I gave her a ride home when I first got my license at sixteen and never thought twice about it again, but she remembered it all this*

133

time. I was in amazement because I couldn't believe she would even know my face thirty-two years later, let alone remember my act of kindness that I hadn't even remembered until that day. What I didn't remember doing, she remembered all these years, and it meant so much to her. The little things we do mean so much sometimes.

But the story continues. My grandson Zakri has a little friend who has a lemon tree next door to his house, and the lady who lives there lets them have lemons. My grandson Zakri has been bringing us lemons from it because he knows I love lemons. Now guess what? I just recently found out that this friend lives next door to the Huebners' house, which, by the way, has one of the Huebner daughters still living there. Mrs. Huebner is in a rest home now, bless her heart, but all these beautiful and delicious lemons we have been enjoying have been coming from Mrs. Huebner's tree. Wow! We have been enjoying the lemons from her tree! Does that not just blow your mind? Is that not just like God to wow you? It wowed me. It's one of those "what goes around comes around" things, even thirty-two years or more later.

> "For we are God's handiwork, created in Christ Jesus
> to do good works, which God prepared in advance for
> us to do" (Ephesians 2:10).

Have you ever had to just sit back and watch something happen when you already know that the outcome is not going to be a good outcome? Maybe it's because you have already experienced it, or maybe it's just because you know in your heart that it's not the best decision, but the person does it anyway. Well, I don't think you are alone. In my opinion, I think the majority of people have experienced this at least once in their lives. If you've ever had an alcoholic parent or child, or drug-addicted parent or child, or just someone who is not making decisions with having God first in that decision, then you know what I am talking about. You have seen something at least close to this. It is a sad thing to watch or be in. What a waste of the precious life we are given.

Sometimes people just don't want to be better. They are happy in their misery, but that's what they choose; it's sad and sickening at the same time. So we just sit back and watch our loved ones choose the world over the Word, and misery over happiness. I don't get it and never will. It is not in my desire or in my design to settle for that. Thank You, Jesus.

I'm still learning, though, every day how to be a better person and know who I am and who I am meant to be. It's a process that will take my whole life to go through. But in the end, I am going to be thankful I tried, and until I move to the next place where I am meant to be, I will not stop trying.

I pray that you will not stop trying either. Life is too short to be miserable. It's too beautiful to be miserable, and it can be so amazing getting signs of love, or as I call them "God-sends" of God expressing His love to you right before your very eyes. It feels like such a personal connection

with the most beautiful, loving, kind, powerful, amazing, life-changing, life-saving Father, a connection that can only be felt and not explained.

The ultimate decision for eternal life is choosing it—or not. But how can there even be a debate in your heart about it? Have you ever had a perfect day or a time when you felt for a split second you were on cloud nine? Would you choose to have an eternity of that day or event if you could? Well, guess what? *Poof*—you can have it! Just choose it. Choose life over death and you will have the desires of your heart. The journey is long and the road can get rough, but with God's love and grace, it will surely be enough.

> *God, through all of the rough edges, and all of the pins and needles, and all of the anticipation, and all of our trials and tests, You are the strength that carries me through. When I get discouraged, You give me courage to face another day of the unknown. But I trust You, God, and I trust Your timing and I trust in Your will. Thank You, Lord, for Your patience with me and for Your love for me. In Jesus' name, amen.*

God is good all the time, and all the time God is good. The Holy Spirit fills what is empty and God conquers the void. In the Bible, it says darkness is no match for the power of light. As a child and even as an adult, I don't care to be in the dark in a pitch-black room because it makes me feel like I can't breathe, like it takes my breath away. When God created life, He works through the Holy Spirit. It is in God, through His Spirit, that we live and breathe and have our being. Without the Holy Spirit, there would be no life.

> "Most assuredly, I say to you, unless one is born again, he cannot see the kingdom of God. No one is born a Christian, and no one is born into the kingdom. That is why it is important and there are no exceptions, that

it is impossible to enter into God's kingdom without rebirth" (John 3:3).

If you're not sure what they are talking about when they say "rebirth," it means that you must be baptized.

"Without the presence of the Spirit, there is no conviction, no regeneration, no sanctification, no cleansing, no acceptable works".

—W. A. Criswell

Of all the things that matter in our lives, it's the study and nature of the Lord Jesus Christ. To know Him through His character, especially His perfection, should be what drives us and gives us the desire to study His Word and get some clarification in our hearts of who God is accurately.

To know God is to have a relationship with Him. To know Him is to brag about Him. God says, "If you are to brag about Me, brag about how I have grown in your heart, show how you are like Me." Do you not want to live life how it was meant to be lived, with God first and foremost?

God doesn't care as much what you do to your body as He cares what you do with your heart. Your heart is God's first concern. God doesn't like when we question His authority and what He says to be true. It should be enough.

Do you ever feel like God is bored with your prayers, or do your prayers seem boring even to you? It could be that you need to dig a little deeper in your heart to feel the Spirit of the Lord. Praying should be spirit to spirit. You can't see anything, but the effects are clear. It amazes me that even though God is invisible, you can still feel Him all around you. You can see Him doing work in your life, yet you can't visibly see Him. That is pretty amazing when you think about it, isn't it? When you think of how holy God is, it makes you feel small, doesn't it? It sure makes me come to understand how little I am.

Why can't we just let God do what God does best (everything) instead of questioning things, like "That guy isn't going to be blessed for acting like that," or "God's going to punish him for that." We need to not go there and stick our noses in God's job. God is in complete control and doesn't need our help to point things out. This may sound like I'm pointing a finger in your face, but I'm not trying to. I'm just saying God doesn't work on our schedule. Let Him take the wheel; let Him drive. This is not our deal; this is His. Our deal will fall short, but Jesus' deal will be sure to win.

Remember, because we exist for Him is the whole reason we were created. We were not created just to get married, have kids, get a good job, and live happily ever after. Those are all gifts from God. When we feel exhausted, tired, and run-down, we will find no rest in life until we find our rest in Him. We are not to be afraid or intimidated by people who have a greater name or more prestige or power, because at the end of the day, we are all the same in God's eyes. We are all going to be judged equally, and this is important to remember.

Don't be overly proud either. It's okay to love your race, but just don't be prideful about it, you know? You're Hispanic because God made you Hispanic, or you're black because God made you black, and so on. That doesn't matter to God.

Unless God has given you something that makes you better than everyone else, then you're no better than the next guy.

Speaking of guys, the only guy that we should be focusing on anyway is "God." He is the one who deserves any and all of our glory. There are scriptures to back it up. Look them up,

I dare you. Do a little Bible study of your own and see what pleases the God you know. Don't take my word for it—I could be pulling your leg. C'mon, look 'em up. You can handle that much.

God is glorified when ... we bear much fruit (John 15:8).

God is glorified when ... our light shines with good works (Matthew 5:16).

God is glorified when ... we refrain from inappropriate sexual behavior (1 Corinthians 6:18–20).

God is glorified when ... we confess our sins (Joshua 7:19).

God is glorified when ... we live by faith and not by sight (Romans 4:19–21).

God is glorified when ... we proclaim His Word (2 Thessalonians 3:1).

God is glorified when ... we stand on our faith when insulted (1 Peter 4:14–20).

God is glorified when ... we do His will (John 17:4).

God is glorified when ... we confess His Son (Philippians 2:10).

God is glorified when ... we reflect the character of Jesus Christ (Romans 15:6).

I have a few suggestions for you of some things you can do to have fun while you learn about the creator of the universe. You can pick a word or phrase, like *joyful*, or *God is glorified when*, or *peaceful*, or *fear not, my child*, or *have mercy on us*. Just think of a phrase or a certain word and see how many times you can find it in the Bible. When you find a word or phrase, jot down the scripture number and the name of the book where you found it, and then see what they all have in common. It's a good way to start learning scriptures, and sometimes they even get memorized and really stick in your brain.

Then, when you need to throw a scripture out there to someone, you have it right there on the tip of your tongue waiting to be spoken. I myself struggle at memorizing scriptures, as I mentioned earlier, but I still try now and then while reading my Bible. What works better for me is to just read the verses slowly and take them deep into my heart and soul and to try and understand them. If I understand them, I can use what I have learned and show what I have learned instead of memorizing and speaking verses. It works for me that way,

Does that make sense? Everyone has their own unique way of studying, reading, and worshiping the Lord. Try different ways until you find a way that feels right in your heart for you to glorify our glorious King. Basically, no matter how you get there, just get there. God already knows what He knows, and there is absolutely nothing He doesn't know. All of the information in all of the libraries in the world, all the data on any computer chip in the world, God knows perfectly and completely because He is infinite. God's understanding is infinite.

That's why, when we are in eternity with God our Father, we will never run out of knowledge because we will never run out of Jesus our King.

God knows your potential history. What if you had been born a different race or in a different era or a different place? What if you had married a different person? Only God knows what could have been. God could have made your life totally different, but He allowed you to be as you are, and He didn't change it because He didn't want to change it. Now don't get me wrong here. I know things happen in life. and certain circumstances arise. I'm not saying God is sitting there letting you suffer through things needlessly by not changing things. It's just that in order for us to grow in faith, we may have to go through unpleasant circumstances sometimes that we don't understand. But God is able to bring good out of even our worst circumstances.

God knows your true motives and thoughts behind what you do or think. Be careful—God is very interested in the intimate details behind the scenes. How does your script read? Would it be something you would want God to act out in your life, or do you need to pay more attention to the fine details of the script that you are to follow?

God knows that we are but dust (Psalm 103:14). He knows we are weak. He knows we can't do all that He commands us to do, even though that ought to be our passion and our goal. He knows we are dust.

God can rearrange things in our lives so they work out for our good, because He knows all things. He knows when we are getting ready to blow it and make that bad choice or decision, or when we are in the middle of a bomb ready to go off, a choice that leads to a life change. *Let go and let God*—remember that phrase? Well, are you practicing it? God knows the best choices to make in the outworking of His plan. It takes intimate wisdom guiding perfect attributes. I'm not able to pull that off. Are you? Only God can do it.

No one could ever come up with as perfect of a plan as the one God can come up with. We probably would have made life a lot more difficult, confusing, and complex, and we wouldn't have been able to take anyone to heaven by sending our son to die for the sins of the world. Would you send your son to die for the murderer in prison or the rapist behind bars? I wouldn't, and I know that I wouldn't. Only God can do it. Our wisdom wouldn't have gotten the job done. God has the superior plan, even though the cross looks foolish to a dying world that prefers to depend on its own wisdom. Don't be foolish, my friend. Let go and let God. He gives free salvation for all if you choose it.

Let God finish doing what He's doing (Ephesians 5:17). "Do not be foolish, but understand what the will of the Lord is". In your time of testing, God will show you how to bring Him glory and show you He wants it in abundance from your heart.

Remember how I mentioned earlier that I could go on and on about Jesus? Well, I surely can. I mean, isn't it easy to brag and go on and on about our cute little grandbabies? *We* love them so much and go on and on bragging, and well, why do we do this? Simply because we love them so much that we can't brag enough. That's the way I feel about my precious Jesus, and I'm going to keep bragging.

Something just came to thought. Does it ever cross your mind of how many titles they call God? Jesus, Lord, God, Savior, King, Father, the Holy One, Higher Power, Sovereign One, and I'm sure you can come up with a few more yourself. Isn't that pretty impressive that someone can have so many powerful titles? Only someone as powerful as God would be worthy enough for that many. Could you imagine being called "God" or "Lord"? I think that would feel as strange as it would sound, calling us "peons" something of that caliber. Sorry for the "peons" title I just gave you; I was just meaning of the level we are compared to God, we are mighty, mighty little, like a grain of sand on the beach—basically, a peon.

No matter how little we are, though, we cannot use the excuse of inadequacy to prevent our service to God. Because we are so little is even better reason to cling to God's promises.

"Be strong and courageous! Do not be afraid or discouraged, for the Lord your God is with you wherever you go" (Joshua 1:9). Sometimes this is what we need to remember when we want to be successful and we want to make a difference in life, regardless of what career we have picked. Sometimes we feel we can't do it because we think we are walking through life alone. Don't feel this way. You are never alone, so accept God's outstretched hand and embrace the power of Jesus Christ in your life. God will always go the extra mile in our lives, but having a relationship with Christ requires something of us. We cannot expect to have a good relationship when it's all one-sided. It can't be a convenience thing. Our relationship must be enduring and committed to God.

Remember, falling on your knees to worship God is not a sign of weakness; it is a sign of love. When we are on our knees before God, our hearts become tender and open for God's touch. Why is it so important for us to look to God to guide our lives instead of reaching in ourselves for answers? Because we need the correct answers of life (Joshua 1:8). Only then will we prosper and succeed in all we do, and who doesn't want to prosper and succeed? If we put God first, we will have unspeakable fulfillment in all we do. As Christians, we will be able to do what God has called us to do because of His great power within us, and when we carry out God's call on our lives, we will find true fulfillment and see lives changed and souls saved.

Let's do a little scenario called "How would you feel?" Okay, so here it goes. How would you feel if …

1. People hated you, but you have loved them from the start?
2. People called you terrible names, but you called them "my beautiful creation"?
3. People called you a liar, but all you have ever said was the truth?
4. People turned their backs on you, but you stood by them for everything?
5. People chose stupid things over you, but you always put them first?
6. People didn't care what you have done for them, but you continue to give blessings?

7. People didn't appreciate you taking the bullet, but you died for them so they might live?
8. People don't want or appreciate your love for them, but you love them unconditionally?
9. People refuse your gift that would last forever, but you never stop trying to offer it?

Okay, so how would you feel if you had these things happen to you? Did you say, "I have"? So you have had at least one or more of these things happen to you in your life? Did you like it? Was it a joyful, satisfying feeling? I'm not trying to be a smarty-pants here; I'm just trying to put myself, or you can put yourself in the way people treat God. Of course, nothing we can call Him or say about Him or not accept from Him changes anything about how He feels about us. How dare we feel anything other than love, even the size of a grain of sand, for our Lord and Savior?

All these things can and will only be handled by our powerful almighty King. No one has or ever will have the power to handle the things that God can. It's a good thing we are not expected to handle these things—thank You, Jesus. He says to give it to Him, that He can handle it. I would be a mess and a raging fool. I couldn't do it; I would want to knock someone's socks off if they did these things to me over and over again. I know that's no way to act, but I am not God and I would go nuts.

Besides, if we leave God out of our lives, we are basically telling him we can handle this life on our own terms. That is not a good message to send to our Master Designer.

> *Lord, thank You for helping me realize that I am weak and powerless and I need You. I realize You are the healer of my heartache. I ask You, Lord, to help me lean on You in times of trials and in everyday life. I realize You are my sufficiency in all things and You are all I need. I commit my will to You. In Jesus' name, amen.*

Sometimes we need more spiritual and emotional help from God than the physical.

God knows us, He created us, and He knows how we humans work. He knows we need to be encouraged and that we need His strength to accomplish the things He wants us to accomplish. God graciously gives us these things when He sees fit to do so. God doesn't leave us alone to face our battles with no direction. He doesn't lead us into something without a vision of moving forward. He wants to give us the encouragement we need to carry on and win the victory.

Just wait until you have a God-send or an encounter with God of your own, and you feel how personal it is and how powerful the meaning is. These encounters could happen every day.

So many times we try to go through life relying on our own visual flight, but God is right there ready to help, just like an autopilot.

It worries me a little that some people think salvation is nothing more than taking some medication and you're on your way to recovery, but it's not. It is not a magic potion that cures all illness. When we are healed, it comes through faith, and faith is a journey that takes time. God is working on each of us, and it comforts me to know that God wants me to be me and wants to nourish me in His own unique way, ways that He has designed specifically for me.

Without God in my life, I would worry about either being in trouble, trying to get out of trouble, or being about ready to be in trouble. Basically, you could say it's nothing but trouble without God.

The Lord doesn't tell us not to worry about our troubles and then not back it up with promises. Joshua in the Bible could count on God no matter what he faced, and the good news is so can you and I. "Don't let your heart be troubled; trust in God and trust in Me" (John 14:1).

Here are a few questions for you to think about, questions to consider:

1. What has been the toughest trial you have had to go through?
2. What is the difference between what God knows and what you know?
3. When have you been in a bind and needed God's help?
4. When has something good come out of something bad that happened?
5. When you spend time in the Word, how do you feel?
6. When you neglect spending time with God, how do you feel?

You do know that we will all be judged, right? I mean that it is God's job to judge us. It tells us several places in the Bible about this. There is more judgment to come, and it's called the great tribulation. Sin must always be judged. Don't you hate when you have a bad day? In those bad days, it's possible to have an outburst when we don't get our way. We judge others for different reasons—anything and everything that is opposed to His holiness.

Here is an important principle for Christian living: when you live your life for the glory of God, you don't have to worry about His love. His love will lead you to glorious places. God's glory will always pick you up and pull you forward when it's time to move. Then He will set you down when it's time to stay. Don't look for God's will. Look for His glory and You find His will.

> "Now to Him is able to do abundantly and beyond all that we ask or think, according to the power within us, to Him be the glory in the church" (Ephesians 3:20–21).

> "Sing to the Lord a new song. Sing to the Lord all the earth. Sing to the Lord; bless His name. Proclaim God's tidings of salvation from day to day. Tell of His glory among all the nations" (Psalm 96:1–3).

> "From the rising of the sun to its setting, the name of the Lord is to be praised. The Lord is high above all nations. His glory is above the heavens" (Psalm 113:3–4).

Here is a little bit of instruction for you that I know my Jesus would want me to add to this book. Remember, I'm writing the story, but my Jesus is the author. He is saying, "Does it glorify My name? Then add it, Teresa." *Yes, Boss, I'm on it.*

Here are some instructions for you. Basically, what we need to do is this thing called "glorifying God." In order for you to follow the instructions correctly, you must first start with step (1): What do you do when you wake up in the morning? You praise Him. (2) When you look in the mirror first thing in the morning? Praise Him. (3) When you eat breakfast? Praise Him. (4) When you get in your car to leave? Praise Him. (5) When you get to where you're going safely? Praise Him. (6) When you arrive back safely from where you were? Praise Him. (7) When you're having your dinner? Praise Him. (8) When you're going to bed at night? Praise Him. (9) When you're lying there and you're still alive and breathing? Praise Him. (10) Now take all of these nine steps and repeat them daily.

If you have a few steps of your own to add, you may do so. Please reread if necessary in order to understand the instructions correctly.

Did you understand the instructions on how to glorify God? If you said yes, then get busy!

Let's do this thing together and glorify our precious Jesus. If you said no, please start again with step 1 and repeat as many times as necessary until the instructions are understood. Jesus loves to be praised and glorified by His children, and He definitely deserves it. Ya think?

Here is a little song I sing around the house or just whenever or wherever I want to sing, really. I just put things together and sing whatever comes to my heart at the moment. Sometimes my songs sound pretty silly, with me trying to rhyme or make it all flow together. But I do enjoy doing it and it makes my heart smile, so it's all good. Even if it's all over the place and sounds like a mess to someone else, I'm having fun singing it to my Jesus.

The song goes a little like this. Oh, by the way, you can put any beat to it. Here it goes:

> Oh! I worship You, my God,
> Oh! I worship You, my King,
> Oh! I worship You, my God,
> And I thank You for everything.
> Oh! I worship You, my God,
> Oh! I worship You, my King,
> Oh! I worship You, my God,
> And for giving me eternity.

Then I sing a couple of more lines of that and more rhyming. Then I sing:

> Thank You Jesus,
> I love You, my Lord.
> Thank You, Jesus,
> I love You forevermore.
> Thank You, Jesus,
> Thank You, my King.
> Thank You, Jesus,
> Thank You for everything.

Yes, it's probably silly, especially my tune or my rhyming. But do I enjoy it? Yes. Does it make me feel happy? Yes. Does my family think I'm a little crazy? Yes, and that's okay, because I am very crazy, crazy for my Jesus! I can sing about Jesus anytime, anywhere, and I really don't care what anyone thinks of it. I know my God is smiling right along with me, and if He is smiling, I'm going to keep a singing!

So plug your ears or start singing!. How does your song go? Is it sillier than mine? I bet it is. I bet you feel so good singing it, don't you? C'mon, don't be shy. You know you've sung in the shower before, so get crazy for the Lord, and start singing!

Get wild, and crazy for our Jesus. He deserves every "crazy" song we can sing. He's worthy of every "crazy" thought of yelling out his name. He's worthy of every hand raised in church. He is just simply worthy of it all. So go ahead, get crazy for our Jesus, It's alright.

What I Always Knew, but Now I Know #19

I used to live in a little two-bedroom house on Fifth Street East in Lancaster, California. In fact, this was the seventh house, believe it or not, that I lived in within a two-block radius. Crazy, I know! I lived in this last little house by myself, but I did have a couple of my kids move back with me at different times for a bit and then they were gone again. It was nice having them there, but it was also nice when they left. I don't mean this in a mean way, but it just meant that whatever the reason was why they were staying there was now fixed, and they were able to move on for the better. So that's what I mean by it was good to see them go. Yeah, right! I'm grinning! Hee hee! Just joking kids. I love you!

I love gardening, or I guess a better word would be "cultivating." I love to grow all kinds of things or bring back plants that no one else wants to mess with. But that's my thing. Well, one day I was out in the front yard talking with my friend Ronnie, and I was watering everything—the flowers, the grapes, the shrubs, the grass—you know, "cultivating." All of a sudden about five or six butterflies came flying around us; they acted like they wanted a drink. They seemed to keep coming closer and closer to the water coming out of the hose and close to my hand that was holding the hose.

I said to Ronnie, "Look at these butterflies. They act like they're gonna land on the hose or take a bath." Then I told

Ronnie, "Watch. I'll stick my finger out and see if one will land on it."

He was like, "Yeah, okay, right!" So I held my finger out like you would do for a bird, and guess what? One landed on my finger! Ronnie looked at me and I looked at him, and we were both like paralyzed, trying to get the butterfly to stay on my finger. I think I can remember even holding my breath, afraid to breathe while it was on my finger. I was afraid to make any movement; I didn't want it to fly away. It wasn't long, maybe a few seconds, and as fast as it had landed on my finger, it was gone. All of them were gone.

Ronnie and I kept looking at each other, and Ronnie said, "Can you believe that? Can you believe that?"

I said, "I told you."

He said, "Told me what?"

I said, "I told you I could get it to land on my finger."

He said, "You didn't know it would."

I said, "Well, I held out my finger and it landed on it, didn't it?"

He said, "Yeah, but it just did."

I said, "Yeah, okay, right!"—the same way he had answered me when the idea even came up.

But he was right; I was just messing with him. I really didn't know it would land there. I was really just being silly, but it really did land on my finger. It was so amazing and almost unbelievable. I'm sure glad Ronnie was there at that moment to witness it. I know he wouldn't have believed me, and I don't think anyone else would have believed me either, being as bizarre as it was.

It's really amazing if you dig into your life history. You can come up with several things that have happened to you already in your life that you can say you were amazed by. Think hard—something will surface in your memory. God sends so many signs to us that we pass up every day by not being in tune with Him. Slow down and take a few minutes to dig deep and think of an amazing moment you have encountered, a real *wow* moment. If you come up with one, then I'm sure you can come up with two and three.

The more I get in tune with God, like I said, the more I can see His signs sent to me. The more you get in tune with God, the more you will realize that things that happen to you and have already happened to you are direct messages from God to you personally, and personally meant for you. For you! Can you believe it? He knows you so well that only God can send such fine detail.

I don't know exactly what the butterfly landing on my finger meant, but there was something to it. All I know is, if for no other reason than if God wanted to see if Ronnie and I would be in awe over it, I certainly was. I can only speak for my own feelings. It did touch my heart in a strange sort of way. It was very special, nonetheless, and I will always remember it.

I think, from the shocked look on Ronnie's face, that he will remember it as well. Sometimes I try to analyze things too much. Okay—honesty, Teresa, honesty! Okay *a lot* of times I try to analyze things or situations too much, like with the butterfly. I try to make sense of things when things don't make sense, or maybe a better way of saying it is when things just seem bizarre. Sometimes it might be better just to leave it alone and accept it just as it is. With the butterfly, I racked my brain trying to figure out God's message. Maybe He wanted to show Ronnie and me an "awe" moment, or maybe He wanted me to buy a butterfly yard ornament. Or, Teresa the analyzer, maybe God just wanted you to be in awe of His marvelous and beautiful creation and not try to analyze anything, but just accept God's beauty for what it is. Nothing more.

Do you ever try to figure things out? Are you an analyzer? I know God wants us to be smart and use our brains, but I get on overdrive probably a little too much. I don't think He wants us to figure everything out. If we knew the reasons why or answers for everything, we would be God, and we are not, of course, and will never be. That's the reason for amazing happenings: so that we continue to seek in Him the answers to the beautiful wonders of the world. I suppose some analyzing is good and healthy for us, but I tend to prob-ably do it a bit too much. I am working on that part of me. I know God knows my heart, though, and He knows I'm just a "Curious George." God's still working on me. Boy—does He have some work to do!

I guess what it all boils down to is this: be in tune with God's messages and signs, but instead of trying to figure things out on your own, pray to God for answers and for Him to show you the meaning of His amazing works. That way, if it is meant for you to know what that bizarre moment meant, then He will show you if you ask. I'm still learning to practice this, and I think I have gotten just a smidgen better. *Eesh*— never-ending work on this girl!

———————◆———————

Life's problems in this world are here and there and have no meaning or purpose sometimes. But when you have the Lord in your life, you have the courage and strength to face these things because God knows that with every random event, He injects a purpose. Again, you may not know immediately the answer or purpose, but be patient. God knows that when the troubles or events have passed, they will leave you stronger and more in tune with waves of the future. Nothing is meaningless in the believer's world. With God, those so-called random things will be turned into good and become perfect and complete with nothing missing.

Life here on earth has its troubles, as we all know. It will have its heartaches, misunderstandings, loneliness, and a loss of understanding the logic of things. But when we depend on the Lord and let Him extinguish the presence of evil, we start to see it pushed back. God's love for us is so much deeper than we know. We can try getting ourselves out of the dark pits of the world, but it will exhaust us for no gain. When we let God take the wheel and trust His driving, He will drive us right out of that dark pit and into light. Which do you prefer?

One of the most comforting words for most of us—I know it is for me—is the word *home*. Home for me is family, comfort, love, familiar, safe, and memories. When I look back at my past, I can picture every house or apartment I have ever lived in, and I can think of something memorable from every one of them. Whether it be a fond memory or not, there are remembered events. But the best house I lived in was the house I grew up in, the only house I ever knew growing up. It is more than a house to me; it holds so many memories for me that it feels almost sacred.

After my siblings and I moved out, we always find our way back home for Christmas and other holidays, and sometimes just for a good ol' visit. My mom still lives in that same house, for sixty-seven years now, I believe it is, and the memories continue to grow. My sister Sheryl was recently here for about four weeks or so. My sister Vickie just left; she came to visit for a couple of weeks. My brother Curtis comes home to Mom's every once in a while. He doesn't care much for Lancaster anymore; things have really changed since he has lived here. It's been a good twenty or thirty years ago, so yes, things have changed very much, and I would definitely say not for the better. Brother Kenny lives in Lancaster close to Mom and comes to see her about once a week or so. I also live in Lancaster, and I see Mom almost every day.

I love when my cousins come over and visit Mom—my cousins Jeannie, Carolyn, and Marilyn. They are all sisters, and Marilyn and Carolyn are twins. They are all so funny and fun to be around. Their dad, my Uncle Jay, just had his nine-tieth birthday. Wow, time flies. My Aunt Virgie is also going to be ninety this year; she and I have the same birthday, July 29. She sure doesn't look ninety. She looks way younger; it must be all the beans and tortillas in her life. My grandma lived to be ninety-seven. My mom will be eighty-eight this year. I'm beginning to convince myself it is all the beans and tortillas in our lives. Of course, it's mostly our Lord Jesus, but the beans helped, I'm sure. I'm grinning!

Man, it just seems like not very long ago we were all so much younger. Time really does go by fast, you know? Too fast! But it's so wonderful, especially when you're blessed with amazing memories of good times with family and friends. But when you think of being in heaven with Jesus and with all your loved ones *for eternity, nothing could be better.* We can all glorify our *precious Lord and Savior* together.

Oh, wow! I get so overjoyed inside when I think of all this that I almost can't even function. It's like it numbs me for a minute. I don't even have a word that could describe the "fuzzy" I feel inside. And just think, that fuzzy is nothing to the fuzzy of what heaven is going to be like. Does it take your breath away just to even try to picture what its beauty will look like and its feeling of *unconditional love*? Oh my! It takes mine!

When my Mom celebrated her eightieth birthday, we had a huge party for her, and this letter was a part of her present. She is such a blessing from God. I couldn't leave this precious letter out of the book because it shows how wonderful and loving God is to give us such a precious gift, our Mom.

We wanted to thank everyone for joining us in celebrating our mother's (Tillie) eightieth birthday. Our intent was to have a fun-for-all party, but we also wanted to make this a tribute to Mom. We entitled our tribute "Mama's Hands," and this is what we came up with.

She used her hands when just a child to hold and help care for new, younger brothers or sisters coming into their completed family of fourteen. Mom used her hands to help propel her little-girl body around the twirling bar at Roosevelt Elementary School, with no care as she showed her homemade broadcloth panties, and to play Ante-Ante Over with her siblings by throwing a rag ball back and forth over the top of their house.

When her dad needed help in the alfalfa fields, Mom was there, sometimes starting at 3:00 a.m. First learning to drive a tractor at nine years old, she used to pull either the bailer or the hay wagon. Mom used her hands as a young woman to learn crafts like painting, leatherwork (making a cow-hide wallet that sixty years later is now worn smooth), and electrical wiring to make such things as a lamp in the exact replica of a covered wagon. As a new wife, Mom bought her first sewing machine from her beloved landlady, Mrs. Linegar, earning the money by candling the chickens, a process using light to size, scan, and separate the fertilized from the unfertilized eggs. While still in her early twenties, and along with Ma Wee and Aunt Ruby, who are among the treasured characters in our family's history, Mom's hands made one hundred beds a day in the officers' quarters at Edwards Air Force Base. What a treat, hearing that memory. When she became a young mother, Mom used her hands to perfect her love of sewing, a hobby and a pastime that has repeatedly blessed her children, family, and friends with that love.

A special memory for me has been watching Mama's hands make scratch biscuits, spooning and tapping them into shape with the tops of her fingers, all baked over the years in the same bent but sturdy little cake pan. Who can count the many biscuits, beans, potatoes, chickens, and tamales her hands patiently and selflessly mixed, cleaned, peeled, fried, and formed over the years? There were thousands of simple but the most delicious meals for her family, made healthy by her love of cooking.

Her hands were used to take us on outings in our childhood days when we all had to accompany her to the grocery store. We kids had to keep our hands in our pockets with the rule to not touch a thing. We had adventures, some as close by as going to the city swimming pool. When I thought Mom was being so kind, I later realized, when I had kids of my own, that it was probably a highly anticipated two-hour rest and reprieve.

On other excursions, her hands prepared sack lunches or cooked meals, and packed us extra clothes as we visited the poppy fields or Little Rock Dam, camped at the beach or in the redwoods, and on the ultimate trips, and probably much to our grandparents' and uncles' dismay, to the Nevada ranches.

Challenging as we kids could be, we've seen those authoritative hands and fingers either snap-point or whack us into shape, often with whatever was handy ... a flyswatter, a hand, a broom, and Curt can attest to a can of hairspray! His scar is evidence. But who cried most about it? Mom did.

Mom's hands kept a decorative and clean home for all our childhood—and even still—while also maintaining her gardens of flowers, pomegranate tree, and at times vegetables, showing her passion and enthusiasm for nature's growing things.

When we kids grew older, she babysat and fed as many as nine kids in addition to her own six. Mom practiced the time-out method of discipline before psychologists claimed and named it. How wise of her to know that separation from the barnyard—excuse me, "backyard playground"—made greater impact than a spanking!

After we all entered school, Mom went to work at the Little Store Market for our Uncle Jay and cousin Freddie. Whether she sold beer, a slice of baloney and cheese for the working men, or bagged penny candy for the kids, Mom enjoyed immensely waiting on her customers of all ages. This included other positions she held at Taco John's, and managing and selling hundreds of trinkets and treasures and trousers at the Salvation Army thrift store. Mom always blossomed when she could be with and serve people.

Our family get-togethers (and for the Ramoses, that means *big*) have always been a source of great joy and pleasure for Mom. Whatever the extent of the work entailed to make it a successful and memorable party, our mother's heart and hands, as well as those of her brothers and sisters, have invariably given willingly and without measure.

Always led by compassion, our momma's hands have driven her to search and find the homeless, giving out coats and blankets in the wintertime, laying aside the fact that in people's desperation situations, they could easily overpower her. When she worked at the thrift store, our brother Ken remembers Dad's frequent remark that he had never heard of someone owing more at the end of the month than their paycheck was worth. Why? Because Mom was buying clothes and blankets for the needy. This is a practice that is now being carried on by our sister Teresa. Now she and her children feed over one hundred homeless people every month, as God allows.

Mom's compassion doesn't stop with people, recently losing her composure when telling our sister Vickie about the death of a homeless and hungry mother dog hit by a car when she was eating from a carcass on the road. Mom instinctively knew that the mother was eating to nurse her now mother-less puppies. This broke her heart.

How many times have her hands been used to call one of us kids? Whatever her premise or reason, Mom's ultimate message is to say "I love you."

Her hands, with the strength of her heart, lovingly cared for our Aunt Jessie when she was sick, our Uncle Doke, Gramma, and Dad up to their very last moments before entering heaven, with no thought of her own grief in losing those so dear to her. Those beautiful hands were also used to symbolize freeing our sister Darnell's ashes to the wind.

Above all, our momma's hands are used daily to turn the pages of God's Word, teaching her so faithfully to praise and thank Him and to love all of us, from great-grandbabies to the homeless and all those in between, in ways that are truly Christlike—generously, graciously, kindly, and gently. Our momma's hands are a beautiful extension of God's heart.

Mom, *thank you* for being *you*!

Dear God, I thank You so very much for the loving and kind mother You have graciously given me here on earth. I couldn't have asked for a better mother. Lord, this is just a smidgen of why I love You. There are so many reasons, Lord. You are perfect in all You do, and this is just another example of Your perfection. I am beyond grateful and thankful, Lord Jesus. Amen.

Some Questions for Thought

Have you ever wondered why this world looks like it's dying? It's because sin kills. Will you choose to live or die?

Is karma real, or is it the definition of Satan enjoying your evil intentions or doings and now taunting you? Will you give in, or stand strong for what is right?

Is it instinct or God? Maybe a nonbeliever made up the word *instinct*. They always say to trust your instinct, but it's more like trust God.

Have you ever imagined you would be born into a dark world? What if the world was ending and you didn't even know? Where is your heart?

Our minds are getting shown evil at a toddler's age so we can be okay with the evil in the world and for what is to come. Don't be fooled, my friend!

Eighty percent of the population doesn't even know what this world is about. Do you? Every day our minds are being shaped by the devil himself. Seek Jesus—that is what the world should be about.

As the generations get older, sin is getting stronger, and the world will die when Jesus is ready. But are you ready to see Jesus?

Have you ever noticed that days and hours go faster, like we are being fast-forwarded? Children seem like they are getting older faster, and we are dying younger. Are you ready for your day?

Seeing is not believing; feeling is believing. Seeing is only what your mind tells you, but the feeling in your heart and soul is true. No one can get into your heart but Jesus.

The next time you come across a homeless person and look down on them, it might be you there in the same place someday. If your income stopped tomorrow, where would you be?

Fear is one of Satan's most popular weapons that he uses against us. The most common lie that Satan uses to instill fear into us is that God is far away or absent from us. This couldn't be further from the truth. Satan is a liar.

Remind yourself of what God's Word promises when it comes to always being present in your life. God will never leave your side.

The presence of bad times is usually the greatest persuasion of God's absence, but remember, God was there even in the midst of war, famine, floods, and storms. God is with us always.

We live in a world full of starving people, yet we are so picky and spoiled, with food wasted in so many places; it's sickening. Try to remember this the next time you say, "Yuck, I don't like that."

Please consider donating a bag of groceries to a homeless shelter or homeless person in your area. Make a difference in someone's life, starting with your own.

We Need Jesus Now More Than Ever

We need Jesus now more than ever.
He healed the blind man and walked on water,
And he raised up Jairus's daughter.
He fed the hungry and cleansed the leper,
But we need Jesus now more than ever.
Jesus, we need You now more than ever,
While we are sailing in stormy weather.
All His children should get together,
For we need Jesus now more than ever.
He touched the lame man and he started walking.
He touched the dumb man and he started talking.
He puts lives back together,
But we need Jesus now more than ever.
In the book of Revelation you can read about the tribulation,
We are heading in that direction.
Only Jesus' blood can give protection,
For we need Jesus now more than ever.

What I Always Knew, but Now I Know #20

My husband, Eric, and I and our five kids used to live in a small three-bedroom house in San Fernando, California. The house used to belong to his grandpa (Papa), and an aunt and uncle also had lived there with Papa.

We had lived there for about two years at this time, and we had redone most of the house. We painted and put in new carpet and just fixed it really nice. Our neighbors were really warm and friendly people, Emily and Ed. Emily was a tall lady, and Ed was pretty short. Ed couldn't hear very well and always had his TV blaring. We could hear it in our house a lot of times, but they were a happy couple and great neighbors to have.

My kids always had a bedtime, and we always tried to stick with it. Their bedtime was 9:00 p.m. during the school week and 11:00 p.m. on weekends. This was a pretty set thing we did. I always liked to stay up after Eric and the kids went to bed so I could have some quiet time and possibly watch some news or something, but I was usually in bed by 11:00 p.m. or so during the week.

During this time while I was up by myself, for about two weeks, I kept hearing a strange sound in the house. It was faint and hard to hear at times, but I could hear something that sounded like socks rubbing on the carpet or something similar to that kind of sound. It was clearer at times, and when it was, it would almost make me freeze with fear. I guess it was fear, or maybe I was just weirded out by what I was hearing. I'm not sure; I just knew that I was definitely hearing something.

This went on for two weeks or so. I told Eric what I had heard, but he thought I was losing it. I told him I was very serious that I was hearing something. I didn't think he believed me, especially by the sound of his voice responding to me. But I knew that what I was hearing was something. The kids got wind of what I had told Eric, and they wanted to know about it. I tried to explain it to them, but they just looked at me like I was crazy. It was really starting to almost make me mad or basically very frustrated that no one believed that I really was hearing something. I didn't understand it myself, but it was something. I could hear the sound go from room to room, and when I would say where the sound was, the house would creak in that specific area.

After about another week or so, I had the kids stay up with me to see if they could hear it. They were all gathered around me like I was a huge pillow. They were hanging on my arms, my neck, my stomach—they were all so scared. I tried telling them that it didn't feel evil or mad. It was just a spirit in the house of some kind, but it was definitely in the house.

So the kids were all around me, and I told them to be very quiet and they might hear it. They finally did, and I thought I was going to pass out with them gripping my body so tightly. They were so scared; they kept saying, "Mom, Mom, Mom!" With each "Mom," it seemed like their voices got shakier and shakier. Now they had heard it for themselves, and they knew I wasn't going crazy.

On another day we could hear a sound like a radio, a TV, or maybe a conversation in the bathroom while the doors were closed. We had a bathroom that had a door on each side, one leading to mine and Eric's bedroom and one to the kids' bedroom. When the doors were closed, we could hear someone or something talking, possibly, like I said, a radio … I don't know.

There were times it was so loud we thought it was Ed's TV from next door, but when we went outside to see if it was his TV, we didn't hear a sound. It was all very strange, but it never gave me a bad feeling inside like it was an evil spirit or anything. It was just there.

A couple of more weeks went by, and now the kids wanted to stay up every night with me. Of course, we said no. Then one night I went to bed—Eric was already in bed and asleep—and I got into bed and was starting to doze off when all of a sudden I saw a white figure hovering over our bedroom doorway. It was shaped like long flowing blonde hair or like a long white gown. Whatever it was, it had me pinned in my spot. I mean, I was frozen with either fear or disbelief of whatever it was that was holding my arm back from trying to wake Eric up. I couldn't move; it felt like I was trying with everything in me, but I was frozen. This thing hovered for a few seconds, and then it was gone.

The second it was gone, my arm hit Eric in the side like I was trying to beat him up. It just walloped him. He woke up star-tled, and I was in shock. I tried to tell him what I had just seen, but it wouldn't even come out of my mouth. Then I started crying. I wasn't getting this situation at all; I was confused and startled, and all kinds of emotions were going through me. What was this, and why was it showing itself to me? I still don't know to this day, but anyway, so now I did not want to stay up late anymore and I didn't want to go to bed either. It was just all so bizarre. What was the meaning supposed to be? Why was I supposed to see this, and no one else? I guess only God will know if this was a God thing. It never felt evil, so I wasn't sure.

About three weeks went by, and then there was the Northridge earthquake on January 17, 1994. Our nice little house was now red-tagged because of the earthquake. "Red-tagged" means we had to vacate the premises and were not allowed back in until it was fixed or a green tag was placed on it. We borrowed my sister Darnell's trailer to stay in on the property to prevent vandalism. During this time of cleaning things up from the earthquake, I came across a painted portrait in the garage that was of Eric's Aunt Linda, with long blonde hair.

When I saw this picture, it gave me chills up and down my body. Was that whom I saw that night? Was it Aunt Linda, or was it a guardian angel? Aunt Linda used to live in the house and take baths in the bathroom in an old claw-foot tub that was still there, and she would listen to a talk show on the radio while she was in the bath. We found all this out later after we shared with the rest of the family what had happened.

When we were ready to move to another house, being as this house needed to be re-built, we got ready to leave on the final day and the girls went up to the window to look in for the last time. As they walked up to the window, the curtains closed right in front of their eyes. That was it. We left and have never been back to the house. Maybe the earthquake was to get us out of there? We'll never know. The house did get re-built by another family, and they continue to live there today. I wonder if they have experienced any of the things we experienced.

I still wonder about that house and wonder what that was all about. This seems to be one of those "I don't even want to try to figure it out" experiences. It was quite the experience—I know that—but this experience was different. The more I gave it thought, the more I felt it probably wasn't from God. I almost feel like maybe the devil was trying to confuse me because the feeling for this experience felt far different from the other experiences I had been through or felt in my heart. It says in the Bible it says to be careful of these types of messages. In other words, do not put your heart and energy into such evil foolishness. It was true what I saw and heard, but it was most likely not of God, I don't know. Therefore, I almost didn't put this experience in this book, but I felt it might help you to understand the difference between a God-send and a possible evil disruption. They do happen, and I have never been pinned with fear with any of the other God-sends that I have been blessed with. Be careful, my friend. The devil wants to get his two cents in there to confuse you. Stay focused on the Lord.

I am so grateful and thankful that I have Jesus in my heart and was able to know the difference between a God-send and an evil disruption. Since this experience, I have tried to stay more and more focused on God and tried to stay in tune. I don't want any more experiences like that in my life. The whole thing was strange, and I don't care to have another one of those.

———————————◆———————————

Have you ever heard that colors have meanings? What is your favorite color and its meaning?

Just a little color fun, from Color Wheel Pro.

Black: bold, rich, power, mystery, elegance, evil, strength

White: goodness, innocence, purity, fresh, easy, clean

Green: soothing, eco-friendly, natural, envy, jealousy, balance, restful

Blue: trust, smart, calm, faith, natural, stable, power

Gray: security, reliability, intelligence, conservative, sad, gloomy

Red: love, immediacy, energy, passion, anger, hunger

Orange: health, attraction, standout, thirst, wealth, youthful, happiness

Yellow: cheer, attention, childish, fresh, warmth, energy, optimism

Pink: tenderness, sensitive, caring, emotional, sympathetic, love, sexuality

Purple: royal, mysterious, arrogant, luxury, creative, sadness

Brown: friendly, earth, outdoors, longevity, conservative, dogmatic

Silver: glamorous, high tech, graceful, sleek

Gold: wealth, prosperity, valuable, traditional

"I alone cannot change the world, but I can cast a stone across the water to create ripples".

—Mother Teresa

"Certain things catch your eye, but pursue only those that capture the heart".

—Ancient Indian Proverbs

"We can easily forgive a child who is afraid of the dark; the real tragedy of life is when men are afraid of the light".

—Plato

"When everything seems to be going against you, remember that the airplane takes off against the wind, not with it".

—Henry Ford

"When one door of happiness closes, another opens, but often we look so long at the closed door that we do not see the one that has been opened for us."

—Helen Keller

"What's money? A man is a success if he gets up in the morning and goes to bed at night and in between does what he wants to do".

—Bob Dylan

"The question isn't who is going to let me; it's who is going to stop me".

—Ayn Rand

"Remember that not getting what you want is some-times a wonderful stroke of luck".

—Dalai Lama

"A truly rich man is one whose children run into his arms when his hands are empty".

—Unknown

"A person who never made a mistake never tried any-thing new."

—Albert Einstein

"I have been impressed with the urgency of doing. Knowing is not enough; we must apply. Being willing is not enough; we must do".

—Leonardo Da Vinci

"Everything has beauty but not everyone can see".

—Confucious

"I have learned over the years that when one's mind is made up, this diminishes fear.

—Rosa Parks

When you hear the word *inspired*, what do you think about it? What do you think it means? In the Bible it means (itself), the very breath, the very word of God. It's the word of God in any form—on a shelf, if you're reading it, if you like it, or if you don't like it.

The Bible is the breathing out of the word of God.

The Bible is unique, unlike any other book. It took more than forty authors to make the Bible up. They came from many different backgrounds, such as tax collectors, politicians, medical doctors, prophets, and a fisherman. It took sixty-six books to make one great book! What's amazing is that all the authors from all over gathered, for the same reasons, consistent messages from God as the source (2 Peter 1:21; Hebrews 4:12–13).

God is alive, and His Word is alive. That's why, when you read your Bible, you feel convicted of sin. The Bible can change your life. It can lead you on the right path, and it can have a penetration that can get below your skin and into your soul and spirit.

Some people say that the Bible was written by men and therefore is a purely human product, and that men aren't perfect so therefore the book is imperfect and there are flaws. But Peter, in the Bible, explains that it was written with God guiding their thoughts. It was through the Holy Spirit that they were able to comprehend the message from God. In other words, while the human held the pen, the Holy Spirit filled in the words through their fingers, but through the mind of God. Even though they had one message, the same message from God, they had many different styles of writing. Basically, when God wanted something in the book, He allowed the vehicle to simply transmit it from mind to pen to paper.

Do you mind if I ask a very personal question? Do you trust God, or do you believe when it sounds good to you? Are you all in or nothing? Too many people want to take apart the Scriptures. They want to say, "I believe that, but I don't believe that," or "That sounds good," or "That doesn't sound like what God would say." But If you can't trust God fully, then why trust Him at all, right? I mean, you likely have people in your life right now that you don't fully trust for some reason or another, so is that really what you want your God to be like? You can totally trust God. He is trustworthy, truthful, and the only one who can save your soul. So, my friend, if there is any doubt in your mind as to whether or not the Bible is true or what God says is true, you, my friend, better get to gettin'! Life is short and time passes fast, so you had better get to finding out what is true before your day is due. I'm just saying.

The truth is like a little fountain. It trickles down from our God the creator, to our Lord Jesus the Savior, to us the sinner and disciple. We must believe this truth to enter into heaven

The best thing about the Word is not only is it true, but it is perfect. Because it is perfect, it reflects the character of its divine author; so it can't be anything but the truth from God. One good thing about the Bible is that it has no contradictions in it. It's the truth, and it speaks perfectly. Remember that it is important to understand that something cannot be true unless it rests on a foundation of truth.

I guess the question is not what's true, but rather, what is the truth? When God speaks, He doesn't blow smoke! That's for sure, because when God speaks, things happen. God's Word is always full of power, and it's going to be brought to us with power. When God said, "Let there be light," there was light (Genesis 1:3). When God said, "Let there be rain," there was rain. Even Mother Nature is controlled by Father God. When God speaks, things happen.

God's Word is also the only thing that can overpower the demonic realm. Many of the negative things we experience come from the demonic world opposing and attacking us. The world is in the realm of Satan's influence (Ephesians 2:2), but even the demons have to obey God when He speaks (Mark 5:1–20). It's kind of like how Dracula was in the movies:

when they put a cross in front of him, he was powerless and ran away.

When people don't know about the right solution, they tend to use the wrong weapon and therefore end up losing the fight. They are defeated. God's Word will either melt the ice or harden the clay, but it will always do something in our favor. It's pretty amazing how the Word of God acts in our lives. When it does find you, it will convict your heart, and sooner or later you will come clean. You can hide from the confrontation, but you can't hide from the truth of the Lord. When the Word of God comes banging on the door of your heart, it would be wise to let it in. It will make you right pretty fast.

There is a fine line to be attentive to. It's very important to stay focused on the lines of life. Just like a football team needs sidelines and a basketball team needs foul lines, in order to play correctly you have to obey the lines. If we didn't have the lines, we would have a big mess on our hands with chaos and lots of trouble (Leviticus 19:31; Deuteronomy 18:11; 2 Kings 21:6; Isaiah 8:19). Take a look at these scriptures and see what kind of message or meaning you get out of them.

"Those who preach must preach God's message. Those who serve must serve with the strength that God gives them, so that in all things praise may be given to God through Jesus Christ, to whom belong glory and power forever and ever (Peter 4:11).

"Now speak the declaration out loud to yourself. The power of life and death is in the tongue, so it is vital that you only allow the truth to come out of your mouth.

It could be the difference in an amazing life and a disappointing one" (Proverbs 18:21).

"For I am sure that neither death nor life, nor angels nor rulers, nor things present nor things to come, nor powers nor height nor depth, nor anything else in all creation will be able to separate us from the *love* of *God* in *Christ Jesus* our *Lord*" (Romans 8:38–39).

"The Lord your God is in your midst, a mighty one who will save. He will rejoice over you with gladness; He will quiet you by His love. He will exult over you with singing" (Zephaniah 3:17).

"Fear not, for I am with you; be not dismayed, for I will strengthen you. I will help you, I will uphold you with My righteous right hand" (Isaiah 41:10).

"I pray that the eyes of your heart may be enlightened in order that you may know the hope to which He has called you, the riches of His glorious inheritance in His holy people, and His incomparably great power for us who believe" (Ephesians 1:17–19).

God's Miracle: Bone Marrow Transplant Day

So there we were—10:00 a.m., Wednesday morning, June 26, 2019, at USC Cancer Hospital, the day of God's gracious miracle, my daughter's bone marrow transplant. I had been taking my son down to USC for the past couple of days to give the bone marrow for his sister, and now was the moment, the gift of life. The procedure is painless and takes about four to five hours to complete. I am telling you, the machine they use is simply amazing, the way it separates the bone marrow from the rest of the blood and the fact that the donor's bone marrow will replenish itself in about three weeks. Amazing stuff, isn't it?

So now the bone marrow was completed, the bags were empty, and it became basically a waiting period to see if my daughter's body was going to accept the foreign cells. It would take about fourteen days for my daughter's blood levels to rise to a normal standing, and when it did, she could not only go home, but it would be a sign that the bone marrow was being accepted in her body.

I am beyond grateful to You, precious almighty Lord and Savior, for Your unconditional love and Your merciful miracles. It is Your perfect plan, God; therefore, it is nothing but perfect. I trust that it is truly just that. Thank You, Jesus, thank you!

There will be a follow-up on how my daughter is doing and on how miracles really do happen in the next book that's waiting to be written.

The Bible is full of praise to God. Here are some scriptures gathered up to remind you of our great God:

"The Lord is my defender; He is the one who has saved me. He is my God, and I will praise Him, and I will sing about His greatness" (Exodus 15:2).

"I will tell of the Lord's unfailing love; I praise Him for all He has done for me. He has richly blessed the people of Israel because of His mercy and constant love" (Isaiah 63:7).

"Praise Him—He is your God, and you have seen with your own eyes the great and astounding things that He has done for you" (Deuteronomy 10:21).

"Praise the Lord who has given His people peace, as He promised He would" (1 Kings 8:56).

"We proclaim how great You are and tell of the wonderful things You have done" (Psalm 75:1).

"Praise the Lord, all the people on earth; praise His glory and mightiness" (1 Chronicles 16:28).

"God is wise and powerful! Praise Him forever and ever" (Daniel 2:20).

"Let us praise God for His glorious grace, for the free gift He gave us in his dear Son". (Ephesians 1:6).

GRACE Bacon-and-Cheese Breakfast Pizza

Ingredients:

½ pound bacon, cooked and crumbled
2 cups (8 ounces) shredded swiss cheese
4 eggs
1½ cups (12 ounces) sour cream

2 tablespoons chopped fresh parsley

Directions:

Roll pastry to fit a 12-inch pizza pan. Bake at 425 degrees for 5 minutes.

Sprinkle bacon and cheese evenly over crust.

In a bowl beat eggs, sour cream, and parsley until smooth. Pour over pizza. Bake for 15–20 minutes or until pizza is puffy and lightly browned.

Makes 6 slices or 18 snack pieces.

Ten Fun Facts for You

1. You can't see your ears without looking in a mirror. (Did you just try?)
2. You can't count your hair. (Don't even try—only God knows.)
3. You can't breathe through your nose with your tongue hanging out. (It's too rough.)
4. You just tried number three, didn't you?
6. When you did number three, you realized it was possible. (Only you looked like a dog.)
7. You are smiling because you were fooled. (Don't be embarrassed; nobody can see you.)
8. You skipped number 5. (Silly you!)
9. You just checked to see if there was a number 5. (Sillier you!)

10. Share this with your friends so they can have some silly fun and be fooled like you!

Did You Know … ?

Did you know the original works of the Bible were written in three different languages:

Hebrew, Aramaic, and Greek?

The first person to be called a Hebrew in the Bible was Abram (Abraham)?

The oldest living person in the Bible was Methuselah, who lived to be 969 years old?

Christ is not a name, but rather a title?

Did you know that only two nuts are mentioned in the Bible: almonds and pistachios?

Pepper is not mentioned, but salt is mentioned forty-one times?

Love is in the Bible 310 times, and *hate* is in the Bible 87 times?

The word *Bible* is from the Greek *la biblia*, which means the "scrolls" or "books"? It's derived from the ancient city of Byblos.

We have all sinned and deserve God's judgment. God the Father sent His only Son to satisfy that judgment for those who believe in Him. Jesus, the creator and eternal Son of God, who lived a sinless life, loves us so much that He died for our sins, taking the punishment that we deserve. Here is a little scenario to make a clearer picture for you.

Imagine you are out hunting with your only son and a couple of your buddies, and you happen to come across some crazy hunters who are out to hunt people, not food. They over-power you, and they tell you all to get on your knees because you're about to be executed. All you can think about is your son kneeling next to you, and you beg the hunters not to kill your son, you beg them because you love your son so much and you see good things for his future.

You had a plan to give him gifts in his life's journey—his first car, college tuition—things that would help him in life. It's already killing you inside to think of these things. Your heart is hurting so badly. You are willing to take the bullet for your son because of how much you love him, right?

Well, my friend, that is exactly what Jesus is trying to tell us, and He did just that. He took a bullet for us because He loves us so much so that we could live and have good things in our future—gifts, true gifts—when we choose to trust that Jesus died for us so we could live for eternity.

Is His dying for you not enough? What is enough? Isn't one of the things we hear people say "I love you so much I would take a bullet for you," or "I would die for you"? Do you really mean that? Would you really take that bullet for them, or are you just blowing smoke? If it got down to it, would you really? If you said yes and you sincerely meant it, you just experienced for a moment in your mind what *God actually did.* Please let the reality of this act sink in. Jesus did for you what you just said you would do for your loved one.

So now what? Don't you want your son to love you back because you love him, and even more because of what you would do for him? Well then, hello! Do you not think our dear Jesus, who did this act for you and me, deserves our love as well? C'mon now! You know as well as I know that every good thing in your life has been given to you because God loves you and has allowed these gifts to be given to you. He would like a little praise and love back for the things He so freely and graciously has done for each of us. He doesn't need it, but He deserves it. Don't you agree?

Do you know that even if you choose not to love Him, He would still love you and desire your love? He continues to love each of us even when we are lost and in total darkness. His love is so patient, loving, and kind that He never stops wanting to give us good things in our lives if we will just choose to love Him back.

How we get to heaven is not a mystery or mysterious information. It's very clear and black-and- white. You can choose to follow the disciples in seeking gratitude, faith, and hope that can be shared and celebrated with Jesus by (1) following the path of servanthood, (2) making the destination a purpose, not a place, and (3) drinking deeply from the offered cup. The purpose is the destination. Don't you want to do the things that glorify our God, and not things that betray Him?

SALVATION Lemon-Herb Salmon

Ingredients:

2½ cups fresh bread crumbs
4 garlic cloves, minced
½ cup chopped fresh parsley
6 tablespoons grated parmesan cheese
¼ cup chopped fresh thyme
½ teaspoon salt
2 teaspoons grated lemon peel
6 tablespoons butter or margarine
1 salmon fillet, 3–4 pounds

Directions:

In a bowl combine bread crumbs, garlic, parsley, parmesan cheese, thyme, lemon peel, and salt. Mix well. Add 4 tablespoons of butter and toss lightly to coat.

Place skin side down in a greased baking dish. Brush with remaining butter; then cover with crumb mix. Bake at 350 degrees for 20–25 minutes.

God, Forgive Me When I Whine

Today upon a bus, I saw a lovely girl with golden hair,
I envied her, she seemed so happy, wished I was so fair.
When suddenly she rose to leave, she hobbled down
the aisle,
She had one leg and wore a crutch, but she sure
had a smile.

Oh God, forgive me when I whine, for I, my Lord, have two legs.

I stopped by the store to buy some candy, the lad that sold it had such charm,
I talked with him and he seemed so glad if I am late it will do no harm.
And as I left, he said to me, "I thank you, you have been so kind,
"It's nice to talk with folks like you. You see," he said, "I'm blind."
Oh God, forgive me when I whine, for I, my Lord, have two eyes.

Later, while walking down the street, I saw a child with eyes of blue,
He stood and watched the others play, he did not know what to do.
I stopped for a moment and then I said, "Why don't you join the others, dear?"
He looked ahead without a word and then I knew he couldn't hear.
Oh God, forgive me when I whine, for I, my Lord, have two ears that hear just fine.

With feet to take me where I want to go, with eyes to see the sunset glow,
With ears to hear what I would know,
Oh God, forgive me when I whine, because I am blessed indeed and the world is mine.

Don't Quit

When things go wrong, as they sometimes will, when the
   road you're trudging seems all uphill,
When the funds are low and the debts are high, when you
   want to smile but you have to sigh,
When care is pressing you down a bit, rest if you must,
   but don't you quit.

Success is failure turned inside out, the silver tint in the
   clouds of doubt,
And you never can tell how close you are, it might be near
   when it seems afar.
So stick to the fight when you're hardest hit, it's when
   things seem worse, don't you quit.

Here are a few gospel songs and their artists that you might
enjoy. I love music.

Vince Gill—"Go Rest High on the Mountain"
Johnny Cash—"The Man Comes Around"
Josh Turner—"Long Black Train"
Porter Wagoner—"A Satisfied Man"
Carrie Underwood—"Jesus, Take the Wheel"
Kris Kristofferson—"Why Me?"
Carter Family—"Circle Be Unbroken"
Hank Williams—"I Saw the Light"
Merle Haggard—"Pray"
Tammy Wynette—"Precious Memories"
Billy Joe Shaver—"If I Give My Soul"
Johnny Russell—"The Baptism of Jesse Tyler"
Louvin Brothers—"The Christian Life"

Does it annoy you like it annoys me when it comes to people saying, "How can God let these things happen?" like Hurricane Katrina or floods or earthquakes? C'mon, which is it? Is it keep God in the schools and workplace and the government, or isn't it? Isn't that what people are trying to do—keep Him out? But yet they wonder why God is saddened by His children to even consider the fact of keeping Him out of anything in their lives, but especially in schools, where we could teach our children about our heavenly Father. But no, they don't, yet God is the first one people call out to or want help from when any of these disasters occur. That's just a crock of crap, if you ask me. Can I say "crap"? Well, I guess I just did, didn't I?

Sorry if that offends anyone. Maybe I should have said it bugs the "fiddle fart" out of me. But my point is, I just get so frustrated when I think about how God must feel when we try to keep Him out of our hearts and other important places in our lives, like schools—especially schools—where innocent children are eager to learn. What better subject to introduce them to than our creator? Then, if the parents choose to continue that knowledge by going to church or reading the Bible at home, so be it. Whatever it takes to learn about our creator and our whole purpose for life and our beings, then do it.

Here is our precious Father, such a gentleman; He just calmly backs out. How can we expect His protection and His blessings if we want Him to leave us alone? So then, which is it again? Is God in or out? I pick "in." How about you?

What about Madalyn Murray O'Hair, the atheist activist and president of American Atheists, who was murdered and her body found a few years ago? Before her death, she went through a brutal heartache. Her family was kidnapped and gruesomely murdered; they were dismembered and then months later Madalyn was killed. I think her heartache must have been insane. Madalyn Murray O'Hair said to take out the Bible in schools and we said okay. Wow! What wrath comes upon us!

Then there is Dr. Benjamin Spock, who said we should not spank our children because it would warp their personalities and could damage their self-esteem. We said yes to that also. Oh, by the way, Dr Spock's son committed suicide. Is it possible that without direction and correcting (Discipline) some important facts of life were not revealed to his son? I guess only God knows.

Now we ask ourselves why our children have no conscience, why they don't know right from wrong, and why it doesn't bother them to kill strangers, classmates, or themselves. Is it no wonder the world is going kaput? People believe a tabloid over the Bible and a man over God. Geez Louise. And isn't it funny how we can send nasty, vulgar things through media and it spreads like wildfire, but send something about God and watch how people are afraid to pass it on in fear of what other people may think and fear of offending them. C'mon, my friends. I don't mean to get riled up, but I do get riled up because this is *wrong*. We were created for purpose and reason, and that all revolves around, through, and for God the creator. If you don't get that even just a little, I will be praying for you in overtime, my friend.

Lord, my God, we need You now even more. Please forgive us for our stupidity and for hearts so cold and unworthy of Your love. Lord, thank You for Your unfailing truth and love, and for loving me even when I act a fool. Please help me to know that Your Word has merit and that it is the truth, and if I discard all the true facts that You've given, I will continue to live in frustration and despair instead of satisfaction and hope. I am free to choose. That's what a gentleman You are, God, Thank You for Your unending love and patience. Amen.

Please look into your heart and do a little soul-searching. Then ask yourself, *What would be the best decision for me to make?* Don't take lightly of the choice. Be careful because there are consequences for the decisions we make.

If you are one of those people who feel this way of putting God out, please don't complain about the world's troubles then. I'm just saying. I mean, if we are not in for God and better, then we have no right to speak about the bad.

So is God worthy of your love and worship? Is He good enough to be in your life just when you need Him? Or is He good enough to be in your life at all times? We've got to go all in or nothing. We can't be hot and cold Christians. God doesn't just love us sometimes; it's always. He never needs us—we need Him. For people to only contemplate loving Him saddens my heart. I love Jesus, and it hurts my heart and baffles my mind. I am just so grateful and thankful that I have the passion to love my *precious Lord and Savior. He gives me that choice*, and *I choose it*. I choose love and eternity over heartache and death. How about you?

When I think about obedience, I think about it being better for me than to stay where I am. I feel that if I am going to hear from God, then I have to listen, and it's going to take a genuine desire to hear from Him. God has spoken to us through those who were inspired to know what the words of the Scriptures mean. His Word is still going forth and speaking to us. But the question is, once again, whether or not we will listen and accept the message of His Word.

On the flip side, God might make you feel that something is uneasy in your life, that something is just not right. You might have that sense of uneasiness instead of a feeling of peace. If you feel like something isn't right, it could be God trying to tell you something. He's trying to get your attention. If you are having some heaviness come your way, it could be that distraction will deafen your ears to the voice of the Holy Spirit. God has His own ways of bringing us to Him, and sometimes the absence of peace is a loud and clear sign that God is trying to get your attention on Him. It's important to trust that God is with us in these moments of uneasiness. It's also important that we trust in God when we're not sure of what direction to go or take.

The Lord will use family, friends, and sometimes a complete stranger. They might say just the right word or do just the right thing that will pierce an area God is trying to get your attention for.

God wants to have a relationship with all of us. He wants to be the number one person we go to when we get ourselves stuck in situations big or little, hard or easy, a yes-or-no situation, or whatever the problem may be.

God will give you the tools you need if you just ask Him, reach out to Him, and create that dialogue. Sometimes we choose to turn to other options, and we forget that God is first and is always there for us. Why we sometimes forget this, I'm not sure. And how can we forget?

God wants to help us and give us resources and ease our pain. So we need to listen for God to speak to us. He will either scream, or talk to us in a very gentle, soft way. Don't ignore or brush it off; these signs could be God calling out to you. If you feel your heart pulling on your brain a certain way, consider it being God's hand in your life. Don't let yourself become so busy that you don't take time to feel the Holy Spirit tugging on your heart.

Over the years, I have had several occasions when I had to decide what I believed God was leading me to or asking me to do. When I really stopped and thought about it, this is what I came up with: *what does the Word say about my situation?* If God's Word is clear about a situation you're in, do what it says. If not, read on.

If you are faced with a similar situation that you have faced before, then what? If God's Word is clear for the second time, do what it says. If not, read on.

If the decision is difficult and you need God's Word to be clear, read (Proverbs 11:14).

If the decision is should you or shouldn't you do something, and you need God's Word to be clear, read (James 1:5).

If you ignore the common sense that God has given you, and you need God's Word to be clear, read (Ephesians 4:18).

Just keep your eyes open for clues and signs. He will send them, and hopefully you'll see them.

———————————————————◆———————————————————

I would now say this book is winding down, but the next book is already starting to unwind. I will keep you updated on the progress of my daughter's bone marrow transplant in the next book I am writing so that I can continue to show you how wonderful, glorious, and mighty God is.

My friends, it all boils down to this: Please open your heart and soul to our heavenly Father. He just wants to love you and do good in your life. Allow Him to lead you to the places He has prepared for you. Allow Him to show you how to deal with life's hurdles. Just tell Him you love Him; He already knows your heart because He created it.

God bless you all, and may your journey of loving our precious Lord, begin right now, if it hasn't already. Get ready—it's going to be a journey like no other!

ABOUT THE AUTHOR

Teresa Kelso was born and raised in Lancaster, California. She attended Belford University, and graduated earning a Double Masters degree in Psychology in Clinical and Counseling. She has also earned a certificate in Private Investigating. Teresa is a freelance writer, fiction and nonfiction, a poet, and soon to be the author of two children's books yet to be published. Her current project is a second inspirational book that will hopefully be out early next year.

Throughout my life I have always loved the Lord and today the only difference is my Love for the Lord has grown even stronger than ever before. I love the Lord Jesus with all my heart and soul, and the Lord loves me and I have proof. The Lord has shown me some real billboard moments in my life, many God sends that show me and proves to me he absolutely loves me. He gives me so many blessings that I am extremely grateful for and the only way to share them with the world is to write them down and tell it so the world can read it. God is so amazing. He is our Creator, our Priority and our Purpose for life. I am grateful and thankful I can tell the world about the Good God we serve. Jesus led my heart to guide my hand to put it down on paper, but the Lord Jesus Christ is the Author of this book on stone.

CPSIA information can be obtained
at www.ICGtesting.com
Printed in the USA
FSHW011057261019
63403FS